NEW AMERICAN SCHOOLS AFTER SIX YEARS

Thomas K. Glennan, Jr.

Supported by
New American Schools

RAND Education

RAND

This report describes the evolution of the program of New American Schools (NAS), a nonprofit private effort to foster significant education reform through the widespread implementation of schoolwide designs. Since its establishment in 1991, New American Schools has contracted with RAND to provide analytical support for the effort. During that time, RAND research staff have played a number of roles ranging from advisor, to field observer, to formal evaluator of the effort. As the evaluations of the implementation of the designs and the outcomes associated with that implementation are completed, the results have been and will continue to be published as separate research monographs.

This report provides a background for these monographs. It takes advantage of RAND's unique perspective to describe the evolution of New American Schools and its strategy for reform during its first six years of operation. As such, it should be of interest to those concerned with the reform of public education and, more generally, with changing public institutions.

Other RAND reports about New American Schools include:

MR-598-NASDC, *Designing New American Schools: Baseline Observations on Nine Design Teams*

MR-729-NASDC, *Lessons from New American Schools Development Corporation's Demonstration Phase*

MR-716-NASDC, *Reforming and Conforming: NASDC Principals Discuss School Accountability Systems*

Lessons from New American Schools' Scale-Up Phase: Prospects for Bringing Designs to Multiple Schools (forthcoming)

Within RAND, this research has been conducted by RAND Education under a contract with New American Schools. Funding to support the evaluation has been provided by the Ford Foundation, the Pew Charitable Trusts, the John D. and Catherine T. McArthur Foundation, and the Knight Foundation.

CONTENTS

FIGURES AND TABLES

Figure

Table

SUMMARY

In July 1991, New American Schools[1] was established to develop designs for what were termed "break-the-mold" schools. New American Schools' initial goal was to create designs to help schools enable students to reach high educational standards. Six years later, this simple goal has evolved into something considerably more complex. The notion of a whole-school design remains at the core of the New American Schools mission. Experience made clear, however, that designs by themselves were unlikely to effect change in schools; training and implementation assistance were also critical. New American Schools thus began to emphasize the role of its Design Teams in helping with implementation, calling this activity "design-based assistance."

This shift in emphasis required changes in the Design Teams. These organizations needed to plan to become innovative professional-service organizations and to develop management, marketing, and product-refinement skills. The Design Teams had not been chosen for these skills and, in many cases, their parent organizations had limited interest in developing them.

Early experience also suggested that wide-scale implementation of the designs would require changes in districts and states. Resources would need to be aggregated to support the implementation. Indi-

---

[1]The organization was originally known as the New American Schools Development Corporation (NASDC). In 1995, it was shortened to New American Schools (NAS), symbolizing its move from development to scale-up design. We will use the abbreviation NAS throughout this report.

vidual schools needed authority to make the changes the designs required. Professional development of teachers needed to be consistent with the needs of designs. Thus, in the last two years, New American Schools has devoted increasing attention to helping jurisdictions develop what it terms a "supportive operating environment."

While working with districts and states to implement designs in a large number of schools, New American Schools and its teams came to understand that there is no regular market for design-based assistance. The Design Teams have developed assistance strategies that engage schools intensely for a period of three or more years. The designs are sufficiently distinctive that significant time must also be spent engaging parents and the community. Implementing a design requires schools and their staffs to devote considerable planning and professional development time to the implementation. The team's fees may reach $50,000 per school for each of these years.

Over six years, the New American Schools initiative has thus developed two key components: continued effort to improve designs and design-based assistance organizations, and the effort to create operating environments and markets in which the Design Teams can effectively sell their designs and services.

DESIGNS

While there is no blueprint for design content among the eight Design Teams, there is agreement concerning the functions of a design. A design articulates a school's vision, mission, and goals; guides the instructional program; shapes the selection and socialization of staff; and establishes common expectations for performance and accountability among students, teachers, and parents. It provides criteria for the recurring self-evaluation that is essential to continuing improvement. It also articulates the student behaviors the school expects and the nature of the work environment a teacher must accept if he or she takes a job in the school.

The New American Schools designs differ in their content. They range from relatively specific descriptions of school organization and instructional materials to broader, less specific visions coupled with a process that will enable a school to achieve its vision. In part as a result of urging both by jurisdictions and by New American Schools, most designs specify benchmarks intended to shape expectations for implementation progress and criteria by which implementation progress can be measured.

DESIGN-BASED ASSISTANCE

The New American Schools initiative advocates an intense, three-or-more year effort by schools to implement a design. A Design Team assists schools in this effort. The team uses its design to provide an initial vision for the school that organizes and gives purpose to the school's entire effort to restructure itself. Experience indicates that schools must have a genuine choice of both the vision and the Design Team for the effort to succeed.

The restructuring effort is intended to engage the whole school. If such engagement is achieved, it reduces the divisiveness often associated with reforms that deal with only a few classrooms or a single subject area. It is also intended to build a school's faculty into a team that shares responsibility for the performance of every student.

The assistance provided by the Design Team is shaped by the design. The assistance is sequenced in ways that the Design Teams have found effective in other sites. If the design ultimately becomes embedded in the culture of the school, it should guide the continuing professional development of its staff and the evolution of its program.

SUPPORTIVE OPERATING ENVIRONMENT

New American Schools arrived at a core set of features that supportive operating environments must possess for design-based assistance to succeed. These features include (1) an effective process for matching schools with appropriate designs, (2) an ability to aggregate resources needed for design-based assistance, (3) a governance structure giving schools authority to implement designs, (4) an accountability process capable of reflecting both student and school performances enabled by the design and the district testing programs, and (5) means for coordinating professional development policies and design-based assistance.

Many of the jurisdictions have been working to improve their operating environments to incorporate these features. New American Schools has begun to develop diagnostic aids intended to help in these efforts.

As the New American Schools initiative unfolds, RAND will continue to evaluate its progress. Of course, the New American Schools initiative is only one of many factors affecting school performance in participating jurisdictions. Leadership, teacher quality, union support, and community support also play major roles in shaping those outcomes. No single evaluation study can hope to capture all the important factors. However, we hope that our analyses will contribute substantially to the public's understanding of this initiative.

ACKNOWLEDGMENTS

In its continued association with the program of New American Schools (NAS), many people have helped RAND. The leaders and staffs of NAS Design Teams and the principals, teachers, and administrators in school jurisdictions where the designs are being implemented have devoted many hours to our interviews and have been unfailingly helpful. We owe all a great debt.

The president of NAS, John Anderson, has been a demanding yet understanding client for our work. His questions and concerns have done much to shape the work and its utility to NAS. All of NAS' staff have helped us along the way, but two deserve special appreciation. Carrie Chimerine-Irvine and the late Elsbeth Kehl have had responsibility for overseeing our work and have provided both encouragement and assistance all along.

This report is the product of the efforts of many at RAND who have shared responsibility for our analyses. Susan Bodilly has directed the field work in both Phases 2 and 3 of NAS' efforts, and her insights and trenchant critiques have shaped much of what is here. Susanna Purnell contributed the understanding of schooling practices gained from her extensive visits to schools and districts. Dean Millot's analyses are the basis for much of what we have to say about the transition of Design Teams to self-sufficient, design-based assistance organizations. Brent Keltner has led RAND's work in identifying the sources and uses of resources for implementing NAS designs. Mark Berends, Sarah Keith, Jodi Heilbrunn, Gina Schuyler, and Robert Reichardt have also contributed to the research underlying this report. Naturally, the author is responsible for any remaining errors.

Chapter One

INTRODUCTION

In July 1991, New American Schools (NAS)[1] was established to develop designs for what were termed "break-the-mold" schools. Funded by the private sector, it sought to engage the nation's best educators, business people, and researchers in the task of creating, testing, and fostering the implementation of school designs that were not constrained by existing regulations, work rules, and conventions. NAS's initial goal was to create designs and associated teams that would help schools enable their students to reach high educational standards. It then moved to implement the new designs in a significant number of schools as an element of a strategy for promoting wider education reform.

This report describes RAND's perspectives on the evolution of NAS's mission. RAND has served as an analyst-adviser to NAS from its beginning. It has also been and continues to be the major evaluator of NAS's program. The perspectives described here now guide this evaluation, and the report thus provides important background for that evaluation.[2] While the report's principal goal is to describe the NAS initiative, it also draws some broad lessons for potential users of NAS's work based on analyses that we have completed and have published or will soon publish in other reports.

---

[1]The organization was originally known as the New American Schools Development Corporation (NASDC). In 1995, it was shortened to New American Schools, symbolizing its move from development to scale-up design. We will use the abbreviation NAS throughout this report.

[2]Appendix A provides a very brief overview of the components of this evaluation.

THE INITIATION OF NEW AMERICAN SCHOOLS

NAS began as a component of America 2000, a broad educational initiative announced by President George Bush and Secretary of Education Lamar Alexander in April 1991. It was the major research and development component of that initiative. In announcing the creation of NAS, the President said:

> We must also foster innovation. I am delighted to announce today that America's business leaders . . . will create the New American Schools Development Corporation—a private-sector research and development fund of at least $150 million to generate innovation in education. . . .

> The architects of New American Schools should break the mold. Build for the next century. Reinvent—literally start from scratch and reinvent the American school. No question should be off limits, no answers automatically assumed. We're not after one single solution for every school. We're interested in finding every way to make schools better. (U.S. Department of Education, 1991, pp. 54–55.)

Other parts of America 2000, including national standards and tests, provisions for school choice, and the development of America 2000 communities, garnered much of the public's attention. When the design initiative was discussed, educators and the research community split on the likely value of the NAS Development Corporation. Many thought that there was already good practice in the field and that capitalizing on such practice deserved higher priority. Others were skeptical about the business involvement. However, many did think that a new school-design effort that put aside some of the assumptions forced by existing laws and regulations had potential value. These perspectives are captured in quotes from prominent observers at the time.

Michael Timpane, then president of Teachers College, spoke for those critical of the emphasis on reinvention of schools:

> It is wrong-headed to suggest that the greatest problem in education is not knowing what to do and that we must wait for privately-funded design teams to come up with ideas. There are many good ideas already in practice including those championed by Ted Sizer, James Comer, Bob Slavin and many others. The problem is learning

how to shepherd these ideas through unwieldy bureaucracies to principals and teachers in every school, people who are just beginning to believe that they can take charge of their professional lives and schools. (Timpane, 1991, pp. 19–20.)

While not totally dismissive of the business involvement in the development of new schools, Gordon Ambach, then and now executive director of the Council of Chief State School Officers, clearly wanted to be sure that the effort was closely tied to the public school system.

I cannot comprehend why the Secretary and the President consider a private research effort to be the centerpiece for system change for the most important function of government—education. . . . Privately funded R&D is welcome but it must be linked with public systems and public authority to be effective. (Ambach,1991, p. 39.)

Michel Kirst, a Stanford professor with wide experience in elementary and secondary education, as well as research, was more positive. After discussing failures in previous government R&D efforts to develop model schools and important research questions raised by the President's proposals, Kirst wrote:

I disagree with critics of the President's program who say that the existing array of schools contains all the necessary variations and we should merely do more research on current promising practices. Schools are highly constrained by various laws, regulations, nongovernment policies (e.g., SAT and the Carnegie units), and organizational rigidity. The New American Schools Development Corporation is needed to break loose from these impediments . . . . (Kirst, 1991, p. 38.)[3]

Having more than $40 million in pledges, NAS put aside the critics' concerns and forged ahead with its program. Three and a half months after opening for business, it issued a request for proposals (RFP) that attracted nearly 700 proposals. In June 1992, 11 Design Teams were chosen to begin the design and development process. A year later, two teams were dropped and the remainder began to work

---

[3]Kirst became a member of the NASDC's Education Advisory Panel.

with about 150 schools to develop, demonstrate, and begin testing their designs in schools.[4]

Two years later, seven of the teams were chosen to move forward to scale up their designs, largely in 10 jurisdictions that had agreed to partner with NAS in the effort. The timetable for the entire program is pictured in Figure 1.1. As the program evolved through these three phases, experience led NAS leadership to change its character substantially.

Phase 1. The initial operations concentrated on the designs and their designers. All the designs were for entire schools. All but one Design Team (Roots and Wings) expected to work with all grade levels from K–12. The Design Team leaders possessed a wide variety of backgrounds, but most were "idea people" and researchers rather

RAND*MR945-1.1*

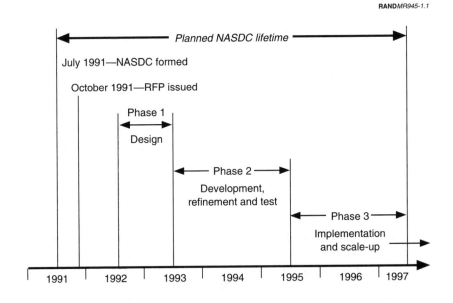

Figure 1.1—Schedule for New American Schools Program, 1991

---

[4]See Appendix B for a description of the different designs.

than experienced managers of sizable operations. The designs were chosen on the merits of the proposals and the team's performance in follow-up interviews. Little or no attention was devoted to whether the organizations in which they were housed—universities, private firms, or nonprofit research and service entities—had any long-term interest in promoting or marketing the design. Most of the teams probably viewed the initiative as a five-year activity, after which the team members would move on to new ventures.[5]

Phase 2. In Phase 2, as the teams began to work in schools, all concerned began to recognize the importance of the services provided in association with the implementation of the designs. In each case, while there were documents and curriculum materials that described the design, the most important part of the implementation process was the provision of assistance to the schools that were involved. Because the designs were evolving, this assistance often involved joint designer and practitioner exploration of problems that arose in implementing the design. As RAND conducted site visits to study the implementation of the designs, it became clear that the assistance was at least as important as the quality of the design itself. In its report on this phase of NAS activities, RAND used the term "design-based assistance" to describe what it had seen.[6]

The shift from primary focus on designs to a focus on a combination of designs and associated assistance profoundly changed NAS's conception of its product. By the end of Phase 2, NAS viewed its primary products as both service-providing organizations and the designs. Because the teams would need to survive after NAS's lifetime, it urged the teams to develop fee schedules and to prepare to move to operations supported largely by fees charged for their services. More generally, it began to work with the Design Teams to improve their marketing and to think about organizing operations to provide assistance to numerous schools. The Design Teams, preoccupied with finishing their design, demonstration, and testing tasks during Phase 2, had little time to devote to this shift.

---

[5]RAND's research related to the results of Phase 1 is contained in Bodilly (1995).

[6]RAND's research on Phase 2 is summarized in Bodilly (1996).

Phase 3. RAND's fieldwork in Phase 2 suggested that, in wide-scale implementation, the NAS designs were likely to face important systemic barriers to implementation. Individual schools needed authority and capacity to change their program and staff as the designs required. Most schools required clear guidance from the districts or the state concerning the skills and knowledge that they were expected to help students acquire. While NAS provided resources for implementation in Phase 2, schools or their parent jurisdictions would need to provide the investment resources needed for the Design Team fees and other costs of implementing the designs in Phase 3.

NAS began a search for jurisdictions that would provide environments in which schools using the designs would be likely to find support—what it termed "supportive operating environments." It sent letters to some 20 jurisdictions (districts and states) asking if they were interested in joining with NAS to transform 30 percent of their schools using NAS or other whole-school designs.[7] All responded affirmatively; 10 were chosen.[8]

The choices were made in March 1995. Because NAS wanted to see its Design Teams in a substantial number of schools in September 1995, a hurried effort to organize new activities in these jurisdictions ensued. It rapidly became clear that everyone had a great deal to learn:

- Organizing a process by which schools learned about and chose Design Teams was very difficult.

- The Design Teams were not well prepared to explain their designs to schools or to state and justify their fees to schools and school districts.

---

[7]The 30-percent goal was chosen arbitrarily. It was intended as a goal that was large enough to ensure that design-centered schools would become more nearly the norm than at present. Thirty percent was termed a "critical mass" of schools.

[8]The jurisdictions were Cincinnati, Dade County, Kentucky, Los Angeles, Maryland, Memphis, Philadelphia, Pittsburgh, San Diego, and an alliance of four districts in Washington. Los Angeles was selected with the explicit understanding that it would not become a formal part of the effort for at least a year and has subsequently dropped out of the partnership. Two additional districts have now joined with New American Schools: San Antonio, Texas (1996) and Broward County, Florida (1997).

- There was normally no ready organizational home in a district or state to manage such an effort.

- Resources to purchase design-based assistance were not readily available in school district or state budgets.

In short, the initial experience of NAS and the Design Teams indicated that there was no regularized market for design-based assistance. If the initiative were to succeed, such markets would need to be developed.

As the extent of the difficulties became clear, NAS itself took a number of actions. It convened representatives of the jurisdictions and Design Teams to address the issues. It hired consultants to work with districts on resource problems and deployed its staff to help with developing effective matching processes. It also required Design Teams to prepare business plans and provide consulting on business planning, pricing, and marketing. By the end of Phase 3, NAS had thus expanded its concerns to include both the success of the Design Teams and the development of districts that were effective in using design-based assistance as a key component of their reform activities.[9]

In the course of the evolution of the initiative, NAS has addressed many of the issues raised by the observers cited at the beginning of this report. Most of the designs have built upon earlier work of reformers in the field. The initiative has begun to address the problems of "shepherd[ing] these ideas through unwieldy bureaucracies. . . ." NAS has worked closely with the education system as it seeks to promote the implementation of its designs. In doing so, it has sought to "to break loose from [the] impediments [of] . . . laws, regulations, non-government policies . . ., and organizational rigidity." (Timpane, 1991.) In the course of this evolution, the initiative has lost much of the simplicity associated with President Bush's initial announcement and has moved to dealing with the messier problems of promoting the transformation of ordinary schools in real communities.

---

[9]RAND will publish a study of the initial implementation of NAS designs in Phase 3. It will appear in the first quarter of 1998.

Table 1.1 provides a summary of the scope of the effort from 1993 to the beginning of the 1996–97 school year. By that time, New American Schools reported that the Design Teams were working with more than 550 schools in about 26 states.

OVERVIEW OF REPORT

As we have noted, this report describes the conception of the NAS initiative that RAND has developed in the six years it has worked with the initiative. It also summarizes some of the lessons that we take from our formative evaluation studies and lays out some of the questions we are investigating in our continuing evaluation of the program.

The report has three major chapters. The next chapter explores the designs and the concept of design-based assistance. It develops hypotheses concerning the potential benefits of such assistance that should be tested as the NAS effort continues.

Chapter Three examines the initial years of scale-up (Phase 3) for lessons concerning the impediments to effective use of design-based

Table 1.1

Schools Developing or Implementing NAS Designs 1993–97

	Phase 2		Phase 3	
Design Team	93–94	94–95	95–96	96–97
ATLAS	13	14	22	53
Audrey Cohen College	4	9	21	17
Community Learning Centers	8	10		
Co-NECT	2	5	19	42
Expeditionary Learning Outward Bound	12	11	23	37
LA Learning Centers	2	2		
Modern Red School House	27	9	16	47
National Alliance for Restructuring Education	81	84	121	217
Roots & Wings	4	4	52	140
TOTAL	153	148	274	553

SOURCE: NAS, November 1996.

assistance. While NAS has moved to assist several jurisdictions to deal with many of these impediments, it is too early for the effects of this assistance to be known.

Chapter Four reviews the problems the Design Teams faced as they moved toward self-sufficiency and greater independence from NAS. These problems have become an important NAS concern as its mission has evolved.

A brief final chapter reflects on the complexity of the NAS initiative described in the earlier chapters and the problems that this complexity poses for evaluators and for those seeking to understand the contributions that NAS is making to school reform generally.

Chapter Two

THE POTENTIAL CONTRIBUTION OF SCHOOL DESIGNS AND DESIGN-BASED ASSISTANCE TO EDUCATION REFORM

The NAS initiative is based on the premise that high-quality schools possess a design.[1] Such a design may be explicitly and carefully articulated, or it may exist as a set of well-developed understandings among teachers, students, and parents that have evolved through time but have never been explicitly committed to paper. A design articulates the school's vision, mission, and goals; guides the instructional program of the school; shapes the selection and socialization of staff; and establishes common expectations for performance, behavior, and accountability among students, teachers, and parents. It provides criteria for the recurring self-evaluation and adjustment that are essential to continuing improvement in any organization's performance. It makes clear the student behaviors the school expects when it accepts a student and the nature of the work environment a teacher must accept if he or she takes a job in the school.

Most schools today appear to lack a design. Rather, they are homes for a collection of activities and programs of varied origins. They typically have some guidance concerning their curriculum, either from their district or from the state. The activities of individual teachers are shaped by their training and experience but are most often carried out in isolation from most of their colleagues. Teachers may independently seek assistance from community organizations or businesses in conducting their classes. Central offices may impose programs dealing with specific subjects or require particular

---

[1]For a complementary treatment of the functions of a school design, see Hill (1997).

organizational activities, such as creating site councils. School leaders may seek grants to pursue activities they feel will benefit their school or their careers. Federal or state funding may require (or be perceived to require) specific programs or practices. In the last several decades, schools have often been required to serve as agents addressing broader societal needs, such as combating drug use or helping young, unwed mothers to begin raising their children. As a result, many schools are essentially fragmented collections of programs driven by both internal and external imperatives.

NAS began its operations by developing an RFP for school-design efforts that would reexamine the assumptions and rules that guide conventional practice and develop designs for new, high-performance schools. At the time, it was not explicitly seeking to develop designs that would help schools possessing fragmented programs to become design based. Rather, its RFP stated it was seeking to create designs for what it termed:

> a new kind of American school—public or private—in which:
>
> - assumptions, about how students learn and what students should know and be able to do, are completely reexamined;
> - visions of the nature and locations of schools are reconsidered; and
> - the manner in which communities create, govern, and hold their schools accountable is redesigned . (NASDC, 1991, p. 9.)

The RFP had several other important emphases as well:

> - the designs were to integrate all elements of a school's life; they were to be for whole schools, not just a single grade or program within a school
> - they were to be "benchmarked" against demanding goals and achievement standards
> - the designs were to be for all students, not merely for those students most likely to succeed. (NASDC, 1991, pp. 20 and 21.)

The RFP thus indicates simply that NAS was seeking distinctive designs for whole schools that would successfully enable virtually all students to meet demanding standards. While the RFP pushed for break-the-mold designs, it also required the respondents to justify their designs through reference to research or proven practice.

The proposals NAS chose for funding envisioned schools that were certainly different from the norm, but they were not radical departures from what was being proposed or practiced by mainstream reformers. For example, no designs made heavy use of distance learning, which was increasingly feasible as telecommunications and computers developed. In fact, a minority of the designs made educational technology a major component of their design. Many of the pedagogical practices proposed have a history in the progressive education movements earlier in the century. However, if the designs did not possess the totally new quality that seemed so much a part of the early rhetoric surrounding NAS, they did appear to have promise to bring greater coherence and focus to schools that conducted their operations in accordance with the design.

The NAS RFP had another feature that reflected its founders' intent that its program be an instrument for the reform of many schools. The RFP stated:

> *This is not a request to establish "model" schools.* NASDC does not seek to develop "cookie cutter" designs. The designs must be adaptable so that they can be used by many communities to create their own new schools. A design team must have an effective plan to generate the energy required for local communities to create their own high-performance, break-the-mold schools. The important thing is that long after NASDC has disappeared from the scene, its legacy of new designs will remain. (NASDC, 1991, p. 21, italics in original.)

One of the criteria by which proposals were judged was their "potential for widespread application and the quality of plans for fostering such application." (NASDC, 1991, p. 35.) While it was not widely appreciated by the NAS staff in the first year of operations, this requirement, together with the organization's subsequent focus on realizing it, gave rise to the emphasis that NAS now places on design-based assistance.

Through time, each team has developed two things: (1) a design and (2) a strategy and fledgling capability for helping schools to transform their operations in ways consistent with that design. Each team's design embodies a "theory of action" containing the implicit and explicit assumptions and explanations for how and why school operations consistent with the design will enable students to meet high standards.[2] The design specifies or guides such things as curriculum, grouping of students, and the nature of the performance that is expected of students. Usually, the design also proposes the broad dimensions of the culture that the Design Team feels is important in its schools.

The Design Team's assistance strategy can be seen as embodying a second, related theory of action concerning the intervention the team uses to help schools transform their operations to be consistent with those envisioned under the design. An assistance strategy guides the sequencing of implementation tasks, the nature and content of the training that is provided, and ways in which implementation progress is assessed and adjustments in implementation are made. The strategy also describes how the Design Teams will relate to schools before, during, and after the implementation of the design.

The designs and assistance strategies have schools as their targets. Recent NAS activities have also moved further to target jurisdictions. As we described in Chapter One, NAS began its third, scale-up phase of operations with the idea that it would seek jurisdictions with existing or planned policies and practices (operating environments) that supported schools that choose distinctive designs and use design-based assistance to implement those designs. It was quickly apparent that the jurisdictions NAS chose to work with were not prepared to use designs and design-based assistance and that NAS itself did not fully appreciate the changes that jurisdictions needed to make to support such use on a sizable scale. Thus, NAS has begun to develop a third strategy and associated theory action applied primarily to a school district.[3]

This theory of action views transformation of schools through the use of design-based assistance as its cornerstone. It argues that the requirement to support such transformations in a significant pro-

---

[2]A theory of action describes the chain of causality that leads the proponents of an intervention to predict it will have positive outcomes. An explicit theory of action should guide evaluators as they seek to understand the reasons for an intervention's impact. See Weiss (1995), Pressman and Wildavsky (1973), Williams (1975), Argyris and Schon (1978), or Argyris and Schon (1996).

[3]Several of NAS's jurisdiction partners are states, but its Phase 3 strategy has tended to be targeted to individual districts.

portion of a district's schools will guide and pressure other district reform activities, particularly those related to decentralizing authority to schools, managing the professional development of staff, and amassing and managing resources needed for school-level reform. If this theory of action proves correct, new district policies and practices, which incorporate schools with distinctive designs and uses design-based assistance, will emerge. The theory posits that such districts will significantly improve the performance of all students.

Thus, the initial vision of NAS's mission evolved to one with three components: (1) the designs themselves, (2) design-based assistance, and (3) a strategy to help districts effectively use the designs and design-based assistance by creating a supportive operating environment.[4] These components are schematically represented in Figure 2.1. They are discussed in more detail in the rest of this chapter.

THE NATURE OF NEW AMERICAN SCHOOLS DESIGNS

In 1991, most observers, as well as NAS's founders, probably expected that a school design would consist of specifications for curriculum and instructional practice, for school organization and governance, and for the manner in which the schools would communicate with parents and others in the community. Most would probably also have said that a design would include either extensive curriculum products or detailed guidelines for the curriculum. Some thought that the designs should explicitly develop or adopt standards and assessments.

However, as noted above, NAS's RFP contained a broader view of the product. The designs were not to be cookie cutters; they would provide guidance rather than rigid prescription. This reflected decades of experience suggesting that completely and rigidly specified designs for education programs seldom were successfully replicated or even sustained in their initial settings. (Berman and McLaughlin, 1978.)[5]

---

[4]The use of the concept of theories of action owes much to discussions with a panel that the Annenberg Foundation established to advise RAND on this evaluation. Its members include Howard Fuller, Paul Hill, Andrew Porter, Karen Sheingold, Carol Weiss, and Barbara Cervone.

[5]McLaughlin (1990, pp. 11–16) revisited this study a decade later.

RAND*MR945-2.1*

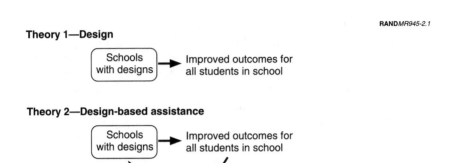

Theory 1—Design

Theory 2—Design-based assistance

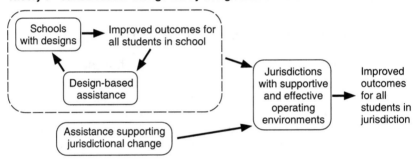

Theory 3—Jurisdictional change led by design-based assistance

Figure 2.1—Schematic Description of New American Schools Initiative

The designs chosen differ in their conceptions. They range from relatively specific descriptions of how schools should be organized and what materials should be used, to broader, less fully specified visions of what the school should look like, coupled with organizational processes to enable a school to achieve that vision. The descriptions of three of the designs contained in the following brief paragraphs provide some sense of this variation.[6]

---

[6]These descriptions are based on materials from the Design Teams' or NAS's Web sites. As a part of its 1998 activities, RAND will trace the evolution of the designs from

Roots and Wings is a design for elementary schools, particularly those serving at-risk youth. It builds on a reading and writing program, *Success for All*, whose development extends back over a decade. The guiding vision of the design is to work continuously to prevent any student from falling behind desired standards of performance.

The Design Team provides both curriculum materials and assessments. Students are tested at 8-week intervals to assess their progress. On the basis of the assessments, students may be assigned to tutors; alternative teaching strategies may be used; students may be regrouped; or other interventions with the student and his or her family may be tried. Class periods for reading are extended to 90 minutes, and cooperative learning is emphasized. A full-time facilitator works with teachers in each school to help implement the design. The facilitator coordinates the assessments, helps with staff development, and generally tries to help ensure that every student is making adequate progress.

Roots and Wings added several components to Success for All. It has a math program that also includes curriculum materials and teaching and assessment strategies. An integrated social studies and science component, called World Lab, has also been developed. Within it, students carry out a variety of projects, often cooperatively. The Design Team has developed extensive materials and guidance for instruction for the World Lab units.

The Roots and Wings Design Team developed its design around the Maryland state education standards that had been set just before the design effort began. The design has little difficulty adapting to other state and district standards for reading and math, since such standards are similar across the country. There have been larger problems with World Lab, because states and districts differ significantly in their requirements for social studies.

The design says little directly about the organization and governance of the school. It does require a family support team to promote family involvement and develop plans to meet the needs of individual students who are having difficulty.

---

what was initially proposed to what is currently being implemented. Our goal will be to derive lessons from this evolution for future reform activities.

Modern Red Schoolhouse is a K–12 design. Emphasizing demanding standards, it uses a fairly traditional curriculum taught using modern pedagogical techniques and substantial amounts of technology. It specifies the character of school governance and seeks to be a school of choice.

Modern Red Schoolhouse began its design work by creating its own standards, which it aligns with local standards, if necessary. It has also developed a set of assessments that reflect these standards. At the elementary school level, approximately half the design's curriculum is based on E. D. Hirsch's *Core Knowledge*, while the remainder involves interdisciplinary units to meet standards related to higher-level skills.[7] The James Madison series developed by the U.S. Department of Education guides its upper-level curriculum. The design requires school faculties to develop pedagogical skills that emphasize helping all students to reach its standards. In contrast with Roots and Wings, however, it does not specify these skills in detail.

The design has devoted considerable attention to management and governance. Modern Red Schoolhouse schools are intended to be quite autonomous, although few, if any, have been granted the autonomy sought by the designers. Training is provided in managerial functions. The design specifies a governing structure for the school that is centered on its design components. The governing structure is intended to engage all teachers in implementing the design.

The Design Team has created a guide to help a school develop a technology plan; technology for both instruction and management is integral to the design. A comprehensive, networked instructional management system is recommended.[8] This system contains information on standards, curriculum units, and student performance. It is intended to support teachers, students, parents, and

---

[7] E. D. Hirsch and colleagues developed the Core Knowledge curriculum based on ideas first put forth in Hirsch's book *Cultural Literacy: What Every American Needs to Know* (1988). The curriculum itself is set out in a set of guides with the title (e.g.) *What Your First Grader Needs to Know: Fundamentals of a Good First-Grade Education* (1997).

[8] The Design Team has not developed this itself. It encourages its schools to choose among several commercially available systems.

administrators in developing Individual Education Compacts (IECs) representing agreements between teachers, students, and parents about student work needed to ensure that she or he meets the school's standards.

Professional development services are provided for the key elements of the design. An important component of professional development is each teacher's experience in writing curriculum units that are based on the standards and focused on developing the skills required to perform well on the assessments.

Expeditionary Learning Outward Bound (ELOB) is less structured than either the Roots and Wings or Modern Red Schoolhouse designs. It is based on a set of 10 design principles that reflect its heritage in the Outward Bound program and govern the operations of an ELOB school. The Design Team describes its general approach as follows: [9]

> Expeditionary Learning is a comprehensive school design that transforms every aspect of a school. Teachers, students, administrators, parents, and community members create a school culture that embodies all of the ten design principles as well as key program components. Students' primary daily experiences are as crew members embarked on rigorous, purposeful, multi-disciplinary and project-based learning expeditions which include strong intellectual, service and physical dimensions.

> Expeditionary Learning schools have significant school-based decision-making and operate within districts where the leadership actively supports implementation of this design. Over time, this design builds community understanding, interest and commitment to public education by offering parents and community members meaningful and rewarding involvement in supporting students' intellectual and character development.

To implement this vision and its ten Design Principles, ELOB describes five "Core Practices."[10]

---

[9]The description of the general approach is from the ELOB Web page in January 1998. The ELOB Web page can be found at:

http://hugse1.harvard.edu/~elob/design.htm

[10]All the quotes are from Expeditionary Learning Outward Bound (1998), pp. 3–7.

1. Learning Expeditions—"[L]ong-term, in-depth investigations of a single theme or topic that engage students in the world through authentic projects, fieldwork, and service."

2. Reflection and Critique—"The faculty is a collaborative of learners who regularly reflect on curriculum, instruction, and the work students produce in order to do their individual and collective work better."

3. School Culture—"Teachers take collective responsibility for the learning of every student and have time to reflect on their practice, and to ask 'Does our school culture make all students feel safe, challenged, and respected?'"

4. School Structures—E.g., the use of block scheduling, heterogeneous student grouping, multiyear teaching, site-based management and decentralized budgeting, shared decisionmaking, and schoolwide reporting and assessment.

5. School Review—"School improvement planning incorporates Expeditionary Learning design principles and core practices and the school's plan for strengthening implementation of them. All school constituencies review the plan annually to assess the school's progress in attaining the Expeditionary Learning Benchmarks, to set priorities and goals for the future, and to approve drafts of the plan."

The design explicitly uses the content standards that are used by the jurisdiction with which it is working. For each of the Core Practices, it provides implementation benchmarks by which schools and others can judge the level of implementation of the practice and, therefore, of the design.

As these three examples suggest, the NAS Design Teams have embraced a spectrum of design conceptions. These vary in scope and grade-level emphasis. The designs range from those that provide clear guidance for classroom organization and instructional materials to those that specify broad principles and key curricular and pedagogical practices but leave the specifics to the school. They vary in the amount and character of specific products they provide— curriculum, training materials, software tools, and materials for engaging the community. Each design provides schools with a vision, but the character of the vision varies widely.

THE CHARACTER OF THE DESIGN-BASED ASSISTANCE NEW AMERICAN SCHOOLS DESIGN TEAMS PROVIDE

Each team also has a distinct strategy for implementing its design. None believe that they can simply hand materials to a school and expect the school to implement the design on its own. Each has distinctive ways to engage a school community initially and different starting points for implementation. They have different ways in which they attempt to introduce quality control.

RAND's fieldwork in Phase 2 convinced us that these implementation strategies shared importance with the designs in determining the outcomes a school achieved. During these visits, the RAND staff assessed implementation progress for each school and probed for the underlying reasons for the progress. Interviews with teachers and principals suggested several important characteristics of the intervention that they thought helped make it more effective than previous reforms with which they had been associated:

1. The design provided a vision for the school that organized and gave purpose to the entire reform effort.

2. The restructuring effort dealt with the whole school, which resulted in less of the divisiveness or fragmentation often associated with reforms that deal with only a few classrooms or a single subject area.

3. The assistance the Design Team provided or that the schools sought from other sources was shaped by the vision inherent in the design.

4. The intervention involved significant amounts of resources, both in terms of the assistance and materials provided by the team and the time devoted by school personnel.

5. Demanding time lines imposed by NAS drove the restructuring effort.

These observations led RAND to place increased emphasis on identifying the *strategies* that the Design Teams were developing to provide assistance to the schools implementing a design, as well as on the designs themselves. Reflecting this perspective, Bodilly, in the final chapter of her report on lessons learned in Phase 2, coined the term *design-based assistance* to describe the emerging results of the investments that NAS had made. (Bodilly, 1996, Ch. 7.) This emphasis is reflected in Theory 2 in Figure 2.1.

While the term "design-based assistance" is new, the concept is not. Many organizations provide assistance in the context of a design. In most cases, this assistance relates to a single program, perhaps in reading, math, or science. In a few cases, the assistance is provided in the context of an entire school. For example, Accelerated Schools and the Comer School Development Program both provide assistance in the context of a design.

The distinguishing feature of the NAS initiative is that it has deliberately set out to develop a variety of design-based assistance organizations with which schools can choose to affiliate. It has invested not only in creating the designs themselves but also in developing organizations and their strategies for engaging and assisting schools to implement their designs.

Differences between school-level reform using design-based assistance and more traditional forms of assistance are portrayed in Table 2.1. The left column lists a number of the elements of school reform, such as the development of a school vision, the acquiring of technical assistance, and the means of gauging progress. The middle column suggests the manner in which design-based assistance deals with those elements, while the last column attempts to characterize the more traditional approaches to school reform. [11]

The entries in the table suggest that the elements of the type of design-based assistance espoused by NAS include the following:

1. A vision, inherent in the design, that guides the school's staff during the design's implementation.

2. An implementation strategy that guides the sequencing of tasks and provision of assistance during the implementation process.

---

[11] Highly effective reformed schools are often the product of exceptional leaders who in fact focus a school's reform effort in ways very much like what the Design Teams try to do. Thus, in individual cases a school may converge on a vision quickly and have a very clear strategy that engages its whole staff. A fundamental premise of NAS's initiative, which serves as a working hypothesis for evaluation, is that Design Teams will be able to help significant proportions of the nation's schools to do this.

Table 2.1

Comparison of Whole-School Design-Based Assistance with Traditional Means of School Reform

Elements of Reform	School-Level Reform Using Design-Based Assistance	School-Level Reform Under More Traditional Conditions
1. Development of a school vision	Starting point is choice of design; evolves through implementation. High standards for all required.	Not required. Reforms typically center on component of school program.
2. Focus of reform effort	The entire school. Seeks to create team with shared responsibility for high outcomes.	Usually subject matter or grades—sometimes governance, e.g., site-based management.
3. Duration of reform effort	Intense initial effort lasting 2–3 years, but reform is continuing process.	No set time.
4. Sources of technical assistance	Initial assistance largely from design team. Long-term assistance from sources deemed most effective by school.	No set pattern. Frequently provided by school district or local teachers college. Training sometimes provided by program vendors.
5. Source of curricular materials	Varies. Some design teams provide detailed materials; others provide frameworks for curriculum development; others use commercially available materials.	Varies according to development of school program. Sometimes shaped by textbook adoption procedures.
6. Strategy for sequencing assistance	Strategy for sequencing actions is explicit. Design teams have different approaches.	None.

Table 2.1 (continued)

Elements of Reform	School-Level Reform Using Design-Based Assistance	School-Level Reform Under More Traditional Conditions
7. Conception of professional development	Professional development is integral to design. Implementation of design results in professional development. Network of like schools is key source of expertise.	Tends to be responsibility of individual staff member. Often dependent on district staff development policies.
8. Organization of staff	Integral to design. Some transitional roles defined. School revises organization and staffing structure to meet its needs.	Tends to be function of district rules. Divided along disciplinary or programmatic lines.
9. Measurement of progress of reform	Benchmarks established by Design Team or by school with Design Team guidance.	Not usually explicit.

3. Assessments of progress coupled with a process for modifying the effort based on the progress.

4. Resources sufficient to enable an entire school to transform itself in a fairly short period of time.

5. Continued support for school staffs in the form of membership in networks of like-minded practitioners and continued association with the Design Team itself.

The teams have distinctive approaches to each of these elements.

Vision Inherent in Design

Our earlier descriptions of three designs hint at the range of visions the designs possess. The vision helps school staff to understand how implementation tasks meld together to produce a transformed school. It should also help students and parents to understand the purposes for which the transformation effort is being undertaken.

In the next chapter, we discuss the difficulties NAS, the Design Teams, and the jurisdictions have had in conveying the key distinctions among the visions of the designs in the process of matching designs and schools. A significant number of the staff in schools report that they did not fully understand the design as they began implementation. This may reflect the reality that a meaningful vision governing school operations is developed6 through experience. Until school staff have actually engaged in the implementation of a design, they may not understand the vision. Moreover, as the implementation proceeds, a school is likely to adopt a vision that is somewhat different from what the Design Team initially proposed. Thus, the vision associated with a design may best be seen as a starting point for a school transformation rather than a prescription for the vision at the endpoint of the transformation.

Strategies for Implementation

The Design Teams vary in the way they initially engage a school's staff, in the ways they provide training, and in the implementation tasks they emphasize. These strategies have evolved and continue to evolve as the teams gain experience during scale-up. Some examples illustrate these points.

The National Alliance, which Bodilly (1995) has characterized as a systemic design, begins by working with both the school jurisdiction and school leadership to develop their ability to analyze their performance against standards and build organizational capacity to help schools improve that performance. As the design has evolved, the Alliance has increasingly emphasized developing a district or state "field team" organized around the Alliance's design components. The Co-NECT Design Team also begins with an activity that is aimed at assessing the school's performance and capabilities and establishing goals or benchmarks for design implementation and school performance but does not engage the district staff.

In contrast, the Audrey Cohen College team works with the entire school faculty for a week before school opens to enable the staff to begin the school year with a distinctive curricular approach and an ability to make effective use of community resources. Roots and Wings begins with a meeting of an entire school faculty. However, this team quickly focuses on its language arts component, Success for All, both because of the centrality of reading to schooling and because it feels that it can demonstrate the results of its approach in a comparatively few weeks, thus gaining support from the teaching staff.

Some of the teams emphasize engagement of the entire school faculty at the start because they want to gain wide understanding and acceptance for the design. This is true for Roots and Wings and ELOB. In contrast, National Alliance and ATLAS have relied more heavily on dealing with leadership teams or lead teachers in a model that trains the trainers, in part because they feel it is not cost-effective to engage all teachers. Modern Red Schoolhouse engages the whole school for some activities but places a lot of emphasis on organizational teams that deal with individual components of its design.

Such teams as ATLAS and Modern Red Schoolhouse believe that school-level governance is central to the operations of their schools and make significant initial efforts to help schools develop effective forms of governance. Roots and Wings and the Audrey Cohen College think it is more effective to focus immediately on curriculum and instruction and move quickly to change classroom practices, dealing with governance as it becomes necessary during the design implementation.

Both Modern Red Schoolhouse and ELOB believe it is important for teachers to develop important components of their curriculum. They engage teachers in intense development efforts designed to help them integrate standards, curriculum, instruction, and assessment. They view this both as an important form of professional development and as a means of developing ownership in the design.

Assessment of Progress and Adjustment of Implementation Activities

Several of the teams quickly developed processes for assessing the progress of schools implementing their designs. Roots and Wings uses an implementation checklist, developed and administered by the Design Team, to provide feedback to schools on progress and suggestions for steps to improve the implementation. Co-NECT makes the development of benchmarks an important initial task and helps the school to measure its progress against them.

Most teams, however, began by providing such feedback more informally. NAS, at the urging of several of its district partners, pressured the Design Teams to develop benchmarks that would serve both to help schools understand what they were expected to accomplish and to provide a framework for adjusting the implementation effort to achieve an improved implementation. While such benchmarks have been developed, our fieldwork took place too early to provide information on their application.

Co-NECT has made a "critical friends" visit an important component of their implementation strategy. This involves a week-long visit by practitioners from other Co-NECT schools to schools in their second year of implementation. The visiting group reviews school operations and makes recommendations of ways to improve those operations. Schools RAND has visited have viewed this as very valuable. The visitors also see it as an important form of professional development. ELOB has been experimenting with a similar program.

Scale-up implementation has only been under way for two years. It is too early to say whether habits of self-assessment, reflection, and program adjustment will actually be developed by schools using design-based assistance. We expect that such habits, if they appear, will be the result of both the design implementation and district policies.

Resources and Time to Enable School Transformation

As noted above, respondents in Phase 2 cited both resources and demanding timelines as reasons for implementation progress. While many researchers and reformers believe that it takes five or more years to reform a school, the goal of most of the Design Teams is to achieve substantial implementation of its design in three years. Most teams expect that the results of such implementations will be increasingly apparent as the design is in place and school operations reflect the tenets of the design.

The sources of resources required to support rapid implementation have been one of the most contentious issues in Phase 3. As we will discuss more fully in Chapter Three, the costs of Design Team services are substantially higher than what districts normally spend for technical assistance in a single school. Some districts have asked the teams to reduce the level of services provided; in the absence of substantial experience on which to base claims of effectiveness, the teams have sometimes been forced to reduce their level of effort.

Perhaps more important than the costs of the Design Teams is the time of teachers and staff to participate in training, planning, and development efforts. In most cases, schools must reallocate their own resources to free the time for teachers and staff to participate in the implementation. They have done so, but teachers have widely complained about the amount of time and effort they must devote to design implementation above and beyond the commitments they have to their regular duties.

Continued Professional Support for School Staff

Each of the teams expects to provide some form of continuing support for staff members of schools affiliated with its design. The teams emphasize continued networking among their schools because of the contributions network members can make to each other's professional development.[12] In this regard, design-based assistance can be seen as one means of trying to foster the communities of professional practice whose value has been emphasized by increasing numbers of scholars and practitioners.[13]

Some teams have been more active than others in actually providing such support. Expeditionary Learning has regular national and regional meetings, as do Roots and Wings and Success for All. Co-NECT also has a national meeting and has begun the development of a Web-based system to provide continuing support to teachers and administrators. Its critical friends activities can also be seen as an opportunity for continued professional development. The National Alliance sponsors a range of conferences and continuing education activities targeted at both affiliated and unaffiliated districts and schools.

For several of the teams, these activities are still in formative stages. The teams have been so busy dealing with the administrative issues of getting started in a fee-for-service business that they have not been able to devote significant attention to this component.

DESIGN-BASED ASSISTANCE AS A FOCUS FOR JURISDIC-TIONAL REFORM

The third theory of action of the NAS initiative, shown at the bottom of Figure 2.1, is both its newest element and the one least well articulated. The key hypothesis is that a district will be required to make significant changes in its policies and practices if

---

[12]Most of the networks center on national meetings. However, the most important network activities may ultimately be established within an individual school district or in compact geographic regions. The Success for All component of Roots and Wings has been available for eight or more years. In several of the districts RAND has visited, schools have already been implementing this design component for several years, and it was clear that faculties in those schools relied upon one another for help and support. Teachers who were uncertain about how to organize a Success for All classroom would spend time in classrooms of teachers in other schools who were viewed as highly effective. Often, a district-level coordinator who specialized in the Success for All design facilitated these visits.

[13]For example, see Talbert and McLaughlin (1994), pp. 123–153.

1. A significant proportion of a district's schools possess distinctive and well-implemented designs

2. Schools implement the designs using design-based assistance.

Under these conditions, it can be argued that schools must have the authority needed to implement a design effectively, that resources must be marshaled to invest in that design implementation, and that the district's professional development will be forced to accommodate and support school improvement. Together, it can be hypothesized that these changes, when coupled with improved standards and assessment systems, will lead to improved student outcomes.

As we will discuss more thoroughly in Chapter Three, the start of scale-up in jurisdictions was hurried. Moreover, many of the jurisdictions lacked the skills and knowledge to embark upon the changes required. As a result, NAS engaged several consultants to help jurisdictions make needed changes. Thus, in Figure 2.1, the jurisdiction strategy involves a combination of the design and design-based assistance and these consultant services.[14]

It is too early to see extensive results of the NAS jurisdictional strategy. Early experience does make it clear that, in districts lacking deep, top-level leadership support for the use of design-based assistance and/or facing funding crises or difficult labor negotiations, the desired jurisdictional change is unlikely.

POTENTIAL BENEFITS OF USING DESIGN-BASED ASSISTANCE AS A CORNERSTONE OF A REFORM STRATEGY

The broad theories of action that we have sketched, if they prove correct and robust, suggest that design-based assistance would have powerful benefits as the key component of an educational reform strategy. The first-level question, whether schools possessing

---

[14]With support from foundations, NAS is developing several aids that districts can use to plan changes in their operating environments. These include an audit of the professional development system, checklists and guides supporting resource reallocation at the school level, and guidelines for aggregating federal resources to support of whole-school reform.

designs leading to program coherence perform better than those that do not, is important, but there is substantial research that supports the idea that the answer to this is positive. (Edmonds, 1979; Newmann, 1989; Newmann, 1996; and Purkey and Smith, 1983.) The NAS initiative provides opportunities to probe this question more deeply. For example, is there reason to believe that designs that provide more traditional structure and prescribed content do better than those emphasizing multidisciplinary and "authentic" instructional tasks? While the implementation of the initiative and the nature of our evaluation design make it impossible to answer this question as well as one might like, RAND will probe for evidence that casts light on this issue.[15]

The principal focus of the NAS initiative and of the RAND assessment has been design-based assistance itself. In this chapter, we have laid out some of the reasons that design-based assistance of the sort offered by the NAS Design Teams might be effective in improving the performance of schools. These include the benefits associated with beginning with a clearly delineated design for the school, support from trainers experienced with the design, and access to helpful colleagues in like-minded schools.

However, there are other potential benefits when design-based assistance is looked at in the context of jurisdiction policies. These benefits, if realized, may provide additional reasons that a district might want to adopt design-based assistance as a cornerstone of a reform strategy in a school jurisdiction. It is possible that widespread use of design-based assistance could lead to

1. *Greater efficiency in the use of district resources for technical assistance.* Intense, total immersion in a guided school transformation may result in more complete and lasting changes in school design. Coupling school-level assistance with the design may thus be a more cost-effective use of jurisdiction resources for assistance

---

[15]A very brief overview of RAND's evaluation is contained in Appendix A. The NAS initiative focuses on design-based assistance rather than on the designs themselves. The initiative emphasizes the importance of schools choosing designs and design teams they feel serve the needs of both their students and their professional development. As a consequence, a form of "selection bias" is created that makes it difficult to disentangle the effects of the designs from the effects associated with the school itself.

designed to improve school performance than are current practices based on salary incentives to induce individual investments in training and centrally designed in-service programs.[16]

2. *More efficient use of instructional resources.* The clear focus provided by the design may help school faculties terminate or reject individual programs peripheral to the design (and ineffective at raising student achievement) and encourage them to devote the freed resources to a significantly more coherent core program of instruction.

3. *More permanent and enduring school improvement.* Schools with clear and widely agreed-to designs may have more ability to sustain their performance through changes in personnel and district environments that inevitably occur.

4. *More rapid improvement in school performance.* The pressure to choose among concrete, competing designs may help schools choose a vision and design more rapidly than they otherwise would.

We emphasize that these are *plausible but hypothesized benefits* of making design-based assistance a major feature of a district's reform strategy. Their realization depends in large part on complementary changes in other policies in a school district. For example, the designs will not help school faculties terminate marginal programs and activities if those activities have strong advocates in the central office who are able to mandate their continuation. The possible benefits of intense, whole-school, design-based assistance will not be realized unless the district encourages and facilitates design-based assistance involving demanding deadlines. The benefits associated with networking with like-minded colleagues in schools sharing common designs will not be fully realized if the professional development policies of the districts do not encourage visits to other sites or attendance at regional or national meetings sponsored by the Design Teams.

NAS's early experiences working with jurisdictional partners illuminated the difficulties districts face in realizing these potential bene-

---

[16]Realizing such benefits on a wide scale requires significant changes in a district's professional development and compensation policies.

fits. These experiences provide some early lessons for jurisdictions considering widespread use of design-based assistance. We turn to them in the next chapter.

Chapter Three

JURISDICTIONAL OPERATING ENVIRONMENTS:
LESSONS LEARNED DURING IMPLEMENTATION

In planning for Phase 3, NAS sought to develop partnerships with jurisdictions that appeared to provide operating environments that would effectively support widespread use of design-based assistance. It sought jurisdictions that would commit to transforming 30 percent of their schools using design-based assistance and hoped that this commitment would lead to jurisdictions in which highly effective schools are more nearly the norm. It also hoped that the business generated in these jurisdictions would help the Design Teams move well along the path to self-sufficiency.

Despite a formal search for jurisdictions with such environments, NAS found that few of the jurisdictions provided a truly supportive operating environment. Use of design-based assistance on the scale NAS advocates lay outside the normal district operations. Funding policies, accountability systems, professional development policies, and site-level management authority and capacity were less support- ive than hoped. As it moved to try to help the jurisdictions and Design Teams, NAS came to see its initiative as involving district- level interventions, as well as the activities of the Design Teams. It began to support work related to the resources, professional devel- opment, and decentralization.

This chapter describes the most important of these challenges:

1. **Matching schools with appropriate designs.** NAS and the dis- tricts were not consistently effective in organizing a process for informing schools' choice of designs. Furthermore, Design Teams

did not provide clear explanations of their designs to schools, districts, or states.

2. **Providing resources for design-based assistance.** None of the jurisdictions had a systematic strategy for investing in the reform of schools, and many individual schools were uncertain about the resources they could draw upon.

3. **Providing school-level authority needed to implement designs.** With the exception of Dade County schools, most principals and teachers did not feel that they had the authority to reallocate resources or make significant changes in operations at the school level needed to implement the designs.

4. **Dealing with perceived mismatch between Design Team curriculum and jurisdiction accountability systems.** Most jurisdictions used fairly traditional standards and assessments for accountability purposes. Most of the designs include curriculum and instruction intended to promote student learning that is not captured by traditional assessments. As a consequence, school-level staff, as well as the district leadership, expressed concerns that the NAS designs, even if well implemented, would not perform well on the existing district assessments.

5. **Coordinating district professional development policies and design-based assistance.** As noted in the previous chapter, design-based assistance is intended to provide professional development for teachers. In the initial year of Phase 3, the school transformation activities were understandably treated largely as an add-on to existing activities. If design-based assistance is to be an integral part of a district's school reform strategy, changes in district professional development policies are likely to be required.

These structural issues were all cited in NAS's scale-up strategy paper. However, the strategy paper was largely silent on another quality of the operating environment that has clearly affected implementation of the designs in many of the jurisdictions: political stability and continuity in leadership. Almost all the NAS jurisdictions faced such problems. Superintendents have retired or are retiring in three jurisdictions; all face regular school board elections or appointments; and several have faced contentious labor negotiations. Several districts have had to deal with serious budget crises occasioned by failures to pass tax levies or cuts in state-level funds. These problems are the norm in American education and, predictably, they often diverted the attention of teachers, principals, and other jurisdiction staff from the NAS initiative.[1]

MATCHING TEAMS WITH SCHOOLS

As was the case in Phase 2, the start-up of Phase 3 did not mesh well with the normal rhythms of the school year. Invitations to jurisdictions to consider participation were sent out in November 1994. NAS conducted site visits in promising jurisdictions in January and February of 1995. Final selections were made in March 1995.[2] By the time the selections were made, jurisdiction and school plans for the 1995–96 school year were nearly complete. Introducing Design Team activities into schools was difficult.

The compressed time periods affected the way in which most of the Design Teams developed relationships with schools. In Phase 2, many of the school sites were chosen because members of the team knew and had worked with an individual in a district or school. Several teams already had established working relations with school systems and built on those. In Phase 3, Design Teams had to deal with schools that did not previously know them and their work. Signifi-

---

[1]Most of the discussion in this chapter is based on interviews in Dade County, Cincinnati, and Memphis. The districts we visited that were part of the National Alliance (Pittsburgh, Kentucky, and Northshore and Everett in Washington state) faced many of the same challenges, but these seemed less evident. In jurisdictions other than Kentucky, the schools were not as far along in the implementation of their designs, a fact that is consistent with the National Alliance strategy to emphasize the building of jurisdiction-level field teams in the first year. This means that some of the issues outlined above may develop in the future. The assessments in Kentucky include performance-oriented components, and Pittsburgh and Washington state are actively moving to develop new assessment systems that will be heavily influenced by their work with the New Standards project. Kentucky provides substantial authority to its schools in accordance with the Kentucky Educational Reform Act (KERA). School-level autonomy was being addressed in other sites but, for the most part, was still in the planning stages in the first year of Phase 3.

[2]As noted earlier, ten sites were chosen, four of which were associated with the National Alliance for Restructuring Education (NARE). In those four cases, much of the initial negotiation with the districts was carried out by NARE. In Cincinnati, Dade County, Memphis, Philadelphia, and Maryland, NAS staff worked directly with the jurisdictions.

cantly, while all the Design Teams emphasized the importance of school staff and parents wanting to work with the team, the fast pace of the early stages of Phase 3 meant there was relatively little time for schools and teams to become familiar with one another.

Table 3.1 outlines the processes initially used to match schools and designs in the four jurisdictions RAND surveyed.[3] As the table suggests, the process of bringing schools and Design Teams together varied for each jurisdiction. Three had some sort of meeting or "fair" at which Design Teams described programs to interested teachers, principals, and parents. Two districts encouraged specific schools to consider one or more models; others relied on administrative processes or informal competitions. Dade County developed a cadre of staff who learned about the designs to help the schools decide whether a particular design was appropriate. On the basis of the Design Teams' positive experiences with these coordinators, NAS has encouraged other jurisdictions to consider such practices.

The unprecedented scale of the effort, together with the speed at which it took place, posed considerable challenges for all parties. None of the partners were satisfied with initial efforts to match schools with designs and modified their procedures accordingly. Because of the importance of the matching process, RAND conducted interviews with nearly 50 principals in Dade County, Memphis, Pittsburgh, and Cincinnati in spring 1996. These interviews, as well as discussions with district personnel, highlighted several problems:

1. Many schools that joined the effort at the beginning of Phase 3 had a poor understanding of the designs prior to making a decision on a design. In most cases, the principal and perhaps members of a site council investigated a design and either persuaded other members of the staff to go forward or made the decision ontheir own. In a few instances, the jurisdiction made the deci-

---

[3]Table 3.1 covers the activities that took place in the late spring and summer of 1995. Most of the Year 1, Phase 3 school sites that were not affiliated with the National Alliance were engaged by these efforts. Since summer 1995, additional fairs or workshops to introduce designs to schools have been held in Pittsburgh, Cincinnati, the Seattle area, several places in Maryland, Philadelphia, and several other areas.

Table 3.1

Approaches to Matching Teams and Schools

Tasks and Functions	Cincinnati	Dade County	Memphis	Pittsburgh
Creating initial awareness	Consumer guide sent to selected schools. Design Teams visited selected schools.	Design Team presentations at New Initiatives fair. Consumer guide distributed to all schools.	Superintendent presentation to all principals. Design literature sent to all schools. High-profile NAS-specific fair for teams from all interested schools.	Presentation of National Alliance (NA) design at summer retreat that included all district principals.
Selection of Design Teams entering district	Central office emphasized certain designs and decided one design was inappropriate for district.	District allowed selection of any design as part of the school improvement process. Technology-intensive design matched with RFP for model middle schools.	Goal was to have several implementations of each of six designs.	Initially, schools only considered one design (NA) with understanding that schools could select other NAS designs after a year of preparation.
Roles of central office staff	Central office staff targeted which schools considered specific designs.	District coordinators associated with each design identified candidate schools and helped them to negotiate to fit design with district policies.	Managed a selection process leading to 28 schools using NAS designs.	Managed selection process leading to selection of 10 schools to begin implementing NA design.

Table 3.1 (continued)

Tasks and Functions	Cincinnati	Dade County	Memphis	Pittsburgh
Allocation of resources	Title 1 at school. Other by central office staff. Schools required to apply for state grant.	Title 1 and reallocation of school-level resources by principal. Patchwork of school and district grants.	Title 1 at school. District administered funds including special appropriation by board of education.	School to reallocate existing funds under proposed decentralization of budget control.
Required participation of school staff in decision to use design.	Agreement by school site council. State grant required 80% vote.	Vote of 80% of staff required by union agreement.	Vote of 80% of leadership team and 60% of faculty.	School submitted application.

NOTE: Based on RAND interviews in December 1995 and January 1996

sion that a school would implement a design or, in the eyes of the principal, was perceived to have done so. This was often the case, even though districts and Design Teams usually required formal votes.

2. Many schools reported that the materials and presentations from the Design Teams did not provide a good picture of the consequences of choosing a specific Design Team. Developing such understanding required extended discussions with the Design Team and, in some cases, visits to demonstration schools implementing the design.

3. Decisions to adopt designs were made with little appreciation of the financial resources and staff time required for implementation. This was true both for schools and district staff and appears to be due, in part, to an initial inability of the Design Teams to state clearly their resource and service requirements.[4]

4. Confusion over the cost of design-based assistance was compounded by lack of clarity concerning resources to be made available to the school by the jurisdiction. In several jurisdictions, schools reported they were promised funding they did not receive.

5. In schools with unhappy prior experiences with "start and stop" reform, principals reported that the lack of clear promises concerning resources deterred selection of a design. In one jurisdiction, some principals reported that their schools were unwilling to become involved with NAS unless the district committed the necessary resources. School staff were unwilling to proceed with a major effort and then "have the rug pulled out from under them."

6. Principals with significant experience in site-based management appeared better prepared to consider design-based assistance. This difference was highlighted in our interviews with principals in Dade County. Dade has had a significant level of site-based management since the late 1980s. Principals there were more conscious of their ability to reallocate school-level resources to support implementation of a design. They also seemed more adept at actively seeking additional resources.

---

[4]The several significant reasons for the difficulties Design Teams had expressing their costs are described in Chapter Four.

7. Perhaps a third of the principals and probably a larger proportion of the teachers did not comprehend what was implied by "whole-school reform." Many schools seemed to treat the designs as another program added to existing ones. NAS has termed this approach to reform "programmitis" and argues that a design should become *the sole* program of a New American School.[5]

The importance of effective processes for matching Design Teams to schools was summarized in a RAND briefing to NAS management. We found that schools visited in spring 1996 reported stronger commitment to implementing a design and to the design-based assistance transformation process when

- The school chose the design.

- The school had a clear understanding of the sources of the resources for design implementation.

- The school was forced to make some hard resource choices about its existing programs so the design was not treated simply as an add-on activity.

- The NAS effort was viewed as a major and permanent initiative in the district.

New American Schools and Jurisdiction Responses to Problems with Matching Schools and Design Teams

Many of these problems can be attributed to the hurried start-up and the participants' lack of prior experience. Design Teams, with NAS assistance, worked to improve the quality of their presentations and refine the manner in which they interacted with schools choosing designs. NAS consultants helped teams develop clearer pricing options. The jurisdictions chose personnel to become more knowledgeable about designs so that they could counsel schools considering implementing the design. NAS provided consulting assistance to several districts to develop their capacity to help schools reallocate

---

[5]While this statement specifically applies to principals and teachers, the phenomenon is more general. Many we talked with in the central office also tended to view reform as made up of a number of individual programmatic initiatives.

their resources to support the design implementation. The district staff themselves, having developed a clearer understanding of the designs and of design-based assistance, began to target more clearly their matching activities to schools they thought could benefit from design-based assistance (while still preserving a school's right to select a specific design).

NAS also provided financial assistance to help maintain demonstration sites. Principals, teachers, and administrators repeatedly emphasized the importance of the Design Teams' demonstration sites in conveying the implications and potential benefits of implementing the designs. The concrete representations of the designs coupled with the opportunity to talk with teachers, administrators, and students conveyed information that could not be gleaned from Design Team materials, presentations, or videos.[6]

Demonstration sites played two distinctive roles. They helped school and district staff understand a design before making a decision to adopt or reject that design.[7] While this was expensive because of the need for many district personnel to travel some distance to the sites, NAS felt it was important to help get the initiative off the ground.

Demonstration sites also served another important purpose. They provided schools that had already begun to implement a design with a more concrete appreciation of the design, the nature of the implementation tasks, and a chance to obtain advice from experienced teachers and principals.

Both these needs for demonstration sites may be more easily met as the designs are more widely implemented, particularly within jurisdictions committed to design-based assistance as a reform strategy. The benefits have been illustrated by the Roots and Wings design,

---

[6]NAS has developed a sourcebook providing descriptions and listings of demonstration sites for each of the Design Teams. See NAS (1996).

[7]In a few instances, the demographic settings of the demonstrations were so dissimilar to those of urban districts that they have lacked credibility. This appears initially to have been the case with ELOB, whose primary sites were in Dubuque, Iowa, and with Modern Red Schoolhouse, whose best sites were in smaller communities in Indiana. Other sites, such as the Accelerated Learning Laboratory school Co-NECT uses in Worcester, Massachusetts, were seen as nontypical because of selective student assignment to a magnet and/or alternative school or the perception that unrealistic levels of resources were available.

which begins implementation with the Success for All reading program, which has been available for ten or more years. In several of the districts RAND has visited, schools already implementing this design component for several years served as demonstration sites for potential adopters. It was clear that faculties in those schools relied upon one another for help and support. Teachers who were uncertain about how to organize a Success for All classroom would spend time in classrooms of effective teachers in other schools. Often, a district-level coordinator who specialized in the Successful for All design facilitated these visits. Design Team and jurisdiction personnel indicated that such activities have already begun with other designs.

Many of the problems discussed here can be attributed to the difficulties associated with starting any new initiative. As the discussion suggests, Design Teams, jurisdictions, and NAS have worked to improve their materials, presentations, and strategies for introducing designs and Design Teams to schools. However, our fieldwork throughout 1996 and 1997, as well as reports from jurisdictions, suggest that schools' decisions to choose and implement a design remain problematic. The difficulty seems to reflect a number of factors:

1. Serious consideration of a design-based transformation effort requires a significant investment of staff time, time that is difficult to find during a school year. Many schools (and jurisdictions new to the effort) do not fully appreciate the need for this time.

2. School faculties are often poorly organized to make the decision to adopt and implement a whole-school design. Many principals lack the skills to engage their faculties in making a decision to implement a design.

3. Schools vary widely in their readiness to implement a design, and the Design Teams are limited in the degree to which they can tailor their assistance to the varied needs of individual schools.

4. Many schools lack the incentive to make the commitment required to implement a design.

5. The complexity of many of the whole-school designs makes it difficult to communicate the implications of adopting a design to a school.

The challenge is particularly significant in jurisdictions that newly initiate a reform effort making heavy use of design-based assistance, since they do not have existing local sites using designs and expertise.

AGGREGATING INVESTMENT RESOURCES

NAS's strategy for whole-school reform requires resources for initial investment in implementing a design.[8] Such investment is needed for initial training and planning, added personnel that some designs require, and materials and equipment. Few schools possess adequate slack resources for such an investment. As a consequence, NAS sought assurances that funds would be available in a jurisdiction to support initial implementation of designs when it chose its jurisdictional partners in 1995.

Jurisdictions do not generally set aside a fixed proportion of funds to invest in school-level reform. Instead they tend to rely upon outside or add-on funding. For example, about two-thirds of the first-year NAS schools in Cincinnati, Memphis, and Dade are Title 1 schools.[9] While this may represent some conscious targeting by the districts, it also reflects the fact that Title 1 provides add-on resources that can be used for training and materials, as well as for additional personnel. In this first year, these districts (as well as those affiliated with the National Alliance) used outside grants from foundations, business partnerships, states, and NAS itself to pay the fees of the Design Teams. To the extent that there is a strategy for investment in reform, it is to be opportunistic in attracting outside funding.

RAND has found no instances of institutionalized district strategies to invest their own resources in school reform. Some states do have elements of such a strategy. For example, Ohio has a venture capital program that has been important in Cincinnati. Washington State also has a program that provides grants for professional develop-

---

[8]School-level investment in reform and the sources and uses of funds for that investment are discussed in Odden (1997b).

[9]Title 1 is a component of what is now known as the Improving America's Schools act of 1964. It provides funds to schools serving large numbers of economically disadvantaged students.

ment to schools. Most of the states in which NAS is working have programs for supporting the introduction of technology in schools. However, local school systems do not seem to think strategically about investment in reform. The lack of clearly identified funds for implementing designs was a concern for many of the schools RAND visited in 1995–96.

The absence of systematic local investment in reform is not surprising for at least two reasons. Since the days of science and math reforms following Sputnik or the Ford Foundation's lighthouse school program, the most common source of funding for reform has been external to schools and jurisdictions. This reflects the fact that most of the interest in school reform has historically come from people outside the schools and school districts. Federal and state categorical programs have provided funding for magnet schools, vocational education reforms, reading programs, teacher centers, technology, and a myriad of other activities intended to change schooling. In their proposals to NAS, most of the jurisdictions cited such programs as potential sources of funding for NAS designs— even though in most instances the funds may have been significantly constrained by their categorical purposes.

Such categorical programs were initiated for a wide spectrum of reasons, including the perception that districts were not able or willing to pursue the goals of the categorical programs on their own. Such programs are now a common element of school finance. As a result, many jurisdictions' reform efforts are governed as much by the ebbs and flows of outside funding sources as by their own strategies for improvement.[10] In our view, responding to these outside pressures has become a behavioral norm for school districts across the nation, particularly those under heavy financial stress. (See Hannaway and Sproull, 1978–79; Hill and Kimbrough, 1983.)

There is a second, equally important reason for the absence of an investment mentality in school systems. Expenditures for schooling are often the largest single category of public spending at the local

---

[10]While such outside funding appears to be the most common source of funds for NAS activities, the superintendents in Memphis and San Antonio (a new NAS jurisdiction in fall 1996) sought and received special funding for NAS scale-up. Whether this will become the basis for a continued investment fund is unclear.

level. The governance of this spending is highly political and public. In such a political environment, aggregating funds and selectively disbursing them to a subset of schools is difficult; the strong tendency is to spread discretionary funds fairly equitably. If schools are to adopt an investment strategy, they will have to find ways to make it politically acceptable to their communities.

SCHOOL-LEVEL AUTHORITY

While initial funding assistance may be required to start the implementation of a NAS design, continued funding for that design is expected to be within a school's means. However, to implement the designs, including obtaining the assistance necessary to continue school improvement, schools must be able to redeploy their resources. NAS argues that schools need control over curriculum and instructional strategies used in a school, consistent with public standards for school performance, as well as power to hire, organize, train, and release staff. This need implies substantial control over budgeting and spending within the school.[11]

Our site visits suggest that most of the NAS jurisdictions are moving in these directions. In the previous chapter, we noted that Dade County has provided substantial authority to school-building leadership. Kentucky has provided substantial authority to schools, and the principals and teachers seemed to be making some use of it. In the other districts, moves are under way, but they are less fully developed. Washington Alliance districts have moved to decentralize authority to their schools significantly. Pittsburgh, with assistance from the National Alliance, is moving to allocate authority over a significant portion of their budget to schools in the NAS program as a pilot project for the entire district. Cincinnati has completed a strategic plan that calls for significant levels of site-based management and allocation of budget authority. Finally, Memphis has put in place a site-based management policy.

---

[11]Such control is less important if most of the resources for reform are from sources outside the schools. To a degree, then, the reform changes are then simply added to the operations of the school. Since significant restructuring of school operations is not required, it is not surprising that reforms supported in this way frequently seem to fade when the external funding ceases.

However, as research suggests, the difference between declaring policies and actually implementing them can be substantial. (Hill and Bonan, 1991; see also Bimber, 1994, and Hannaway and Carnoy, 1993.) In particular, authority at the school level is often limited by state and district policies governing personnel and curriculum, provisions of labor agreements with teachers and other district staff, and the unwillingness of central office staff to relinquish control (often coupled with district reluctance to reduce the size and authority of that staff).

While legal and policy authority are important and may even have been provided, many school personnel do not know how to use it. Some Design Teams (e.g., Modern Red Schoolhouse, Co-NECT, and ATLAS) provide specific training on site-level management to school staffs implementing their designs. NAS has also considered developing a curriculum unit that would prepare schools to assume this authority.[12]

In summary, our site visits suggest that, in most districts, much remains to be done to decentralize authority and responsibility for allocating school-level resources, shaping instructional programs, and developing schools' capability to use that authority. However, in most districts, significant initiatives are under way.[13]

LACK OF ALIGNMENT OF DESIGNS WITH JURISDICTION ACCOUNTABILITY SYSTEMS

Across the nation, states and districts are in the midst of major efforts to develop high standards together with supporting curricular frameworks and assessment systems. However, few have been put in

---

[12]Roots and Wings provides a distinctive example. It tends to operate only in Title 1 schools where substantial additional funding is available and where the principals and district Title 1 coordinators have substantial discretion over funding allocations. The Roots and Wings staff have developed a number of models for reallocating those resources to cover the costs of implementing their program. This is possible because the funding supplements normal school funds and is largely governed by federal regulations supportive of such flexibility.

[13]Allen Odden, with support from NAS, has provided advice on decentralization to several jurisdictions. See Odden (1997a).

place, and considerable controversy still surrounds the assessments.[14]

Consequently, many of the Design Teams are working in jurisdictions where the outcomes of their implementation will be judged, in part, by existing accountability systems. A major feature of such systems is scores on tests mandated by the state or the district and comprising mainly multiple-choice questions emphasizing basic skills or specific content.

Both school and jurisdiction personnel were concerned that the designs would not rapidly improve test scores on these tests. In our interviews, both in Phase 2 and Phase 3, most schools and teachers "stepped out" of the designs to do some preparation for tests. This was the case in Phase 2 schools, even though the majority of the principals interviewed had had positive growths in scores in the past.[15]

In Phase 3, principals and teachers in several of the jurisdictions pointedly—even angrily—complained that they were being strongly encouraged to use new designs (often because their schools had poor performance on existing tests). However, they were concerned that these designs were not keyed to improving scores quickly on the more traditional tests that continue to be emphasized in the jurisdiction's accountability system. Moreover, in several districts, performance on mandated tests was a component of systems for evaluating performance of school-level personnel.

To deal with the test-alignment problem, several of the Design Teams proposed administering a separate assessment that had both components from current jurisdiction assessments and items from more modern performance assessments. The results would be reported to the public as a supplement to the existing testing program. In a NAS working group, made up of both jurisdiction and

---

[14]Several of the NAS Design Teams have devoted effort to this issue. NARE is associated with New Standards, a major effort to develop standards and assessments. National Alliance districts are either beginning to use this assessment system or developing and using systems that are broadly consistent (e.g., Kentucky assessments). Modern Red Schoolhouse has also developed its own assessments for determining whether students are prepared to move from one broad schooling level to another.

[15]These interviews are described in Mitchell (1996).

Design Team personnel, the jurisdiction personnel strongly rejected such an assessment as too expensive and confusing and politically infeasible. Moreover, some felt it was unclear that such an assessment would relieve the teachers' and parents' anxieties concerning the possibility of poor performance on the mainstream jurisdiction assessments.

As this is written, alignment of designs with accountability systems continues to be a vexing problem. The jurisdiction leaders feel that the schools using the designs must improve on traditional measures in addition to fostering student skills not measured by their tests. The Design Teams are concerned that their schools will be slow to do well on such assessments but, more importantly, many worry that if schools insist on continuing to prepare for the regular assessments, it will seriously set back implementation efforts. There is pressure in some districts for Design Teams that lack explicit reading programs to incorporate such programs in their designs.

PROFESSIONAL DEVELOPMENT

The professional development of teachers is obviously central to the improvement of student performance. However, there is broad agreement that current practices promoting professional development leave much to be desired. For example, the report of the National Commission on Teaching and America's Future quotes one expert who says:

> A good deal of what passes for "professional development" in schools is a joke—one that we'd laugh at if we weren't trying to keep from crying. It's everything that a learning environment shouldn't be: radically under-resourced, brief, not sustained, designed for "one-size-fits-all," imposed rather than owned, lacking intellectual coherence, treated as a special add-on rather than as part of a natural process, and trapped in the constraints of the bureaucratic system we have come to call "school." In short, it's pedagogically naïve, a demeaning exercise that often leaves its participants more cynical and not more knowledgeable, skilled, or committed than before. (Miles, 1995.)

Miles goes on to note that not all professional development is like that, however, so there "may be hope." In that vein, the design-based assistance NAS supports is intended to deal with each of the problems listed in the quotation. Professional development of teachers is the center point of all of the NAS designs. Design Teams promote it in a variety of ways, through direct training, by sponsoring design network conferences, by providing coaching and opportunities to observe experts, by guiding planning activities, or by requiring teachers to develop curriculum units. A tenet of all the designs is that professional development should be continuing rather than restricted to discrete episodes.

However, the Design Teams have been thrust into jurisdictions with a wide range of existing professional development practices that seem quite fragmented. There are some attempts to change. Cincinnati and Memphis are both in the midst of building professional development centers. Kentucky has several regional centers providing professional development opportunities, and the beginnings of such centers exist in the Seattle area. In all the local jurisdictions, central offices still run in-services and mandate staff-development activities that are often not central to the requirements of the schools.

Perhaps the policy that provides the greatest impetus to professional development of school-level personnel is the reward structure that is built into a district's salary schedule. The jurisdictions we visited currently have traditional pay schedules in which pay is based on credit hours of education and length of service, leaving decisions concerning what courses should be taken and what experience should be gained largely to individual teachers and school-level professional staff. With the exception of Kentucky, which provides cash awards to schools performing well, none of the jurisdictions currently provide rewards based on performance.

While the hurried start-up in Phase 3 made coordination of design-based assistance and other professional development activities difficult, there were several examples of district-sponsored professional development activities that may have supported the implementation of designs. Districts have provided training in site-based management and budget planning; instructional approaches, such as cooperative learning; and the development of skills related to the use of technology.

District funds for professional development were used to pay for some of the costs of implementing designs. RAND's preliminary analysis of sources of resources for school transformation found that districts have made extensive use of professional development funds to release time for teachers and, in a few instances, to provide stipends for time spent in summer retreats or other staff development activities.

The site visits also suggested that district personnel could contribute significantly to the utilization of design-based assistance. Dade County assigned district staff to become experts on a design, assist schools to decide whether a design was appropriate for them, and coordinate the relations between the Design Team and the district. The Design Teams found this helpful and have recommended that the practice be extended to other jurisdictions. In Memphis, the Teaching and Learning Center is responsible for the NAS effort, and its staff coordinates the efforts of Design Teams and schools. Both these examples provide beginning models for the integration of design-based assistance with district professional development.

While meshing design-based assistance with other professional development efforts has begun, many important issues remain. For example,

1. Several of the jurisdictions want to substitute district staff for Design Team trainers, in large part because they are viewed as less expensive. These districts would like to have the Design Teams help them build their internal capacity to extend the designs. Since they depend on fees for training services, Design Teams have little incentive to make such a move.

2. Little attention has been given to the roles of the Design Team after the initial school transformation has taken place. Should the teams play a continuing role in providing quality control? Should they provide on-call assistance and troubleshooting? Will their primary function be to maintain and nurture a network of practitioners sharing an interest in their design? Neither the teams, schools, nor jurisdictions have fully developed answers to these questions.

3. Many of the designs share a number of common instructional themes, such as the use of project-based learning, multiage

grouping, and looping (teachers spending several years rather than a single year with a class). Can the recruiting practices of a district and its association with its primary sources of teachers be used to ensure that new teachers arrive in the classroom equipped with some of the pedagogical skills needed by the designs?

These issues share a common thread. The goal of the NAS initiative is to create schools whose faculties perform as teams focusing on continually improving their students' performance. The initiative envisions schools themselves having the responsibility to organize their professional development activities so that they contribute to the performance of the school. It also envisions a system in which incentives, including those associated with the determination of salary, reinforce this overall goal.

The long-term success of design-based assistance as an instrument of reform and improvement depends upon making it an integral part of all the policies shaping the professional development of a jurisdiction's staff. Recognizing this, NAS is collaborating with several jurisdictions to analyze professional development needs and design more-effective policies.[16]

---

[16]The ideas shaping this work are described in Haslam (1997). Haslam's paper begins with his review of lessons he takes from NAS's initial year of scale-up.

Chapter Four

CHALLENGES FOR DESIGN TEAMS SEEKING
SELF-SUFFICIENCY

The lasting contribution of NAS to the reform of American schools requires its Design Teams to achieve self-sufficiency so that they can continue to help schools to implement their designs. As we noted in earlier chapters, NAS has done this by assisting the teams to move from dependence on grants[1] to a level of independent operations where fees for services and products will be sufficient to cover their costs. Several of the teams that existed prior to their affiliation with NAS have achieved a level of self-sufficiency; for most, the future remains uncertain, if promising.[2]

The importance of the teams becoming self-sufficient means NAS has taken on qualities of a venture capitalist, investing in the development of new products and services and new organizations. However, it did not begin with this perspective. In choosing the organizations in which to invest, it gave very little attention to their underlying financial and management capabilities. Instead, NAS concentrated on choosing groups with design concepts with the most potential for improving schools and student achievement. It invested in the development of a product but, until the past two years, paid little attention to other capabilities of the enterprise necessary to its success.

---

[1]The support was actually provided through contracts, but NAS managed them in ways similar to foundation grants.

[2]The two whose futures seem most assured at this writing are Roots and Wings and the National Alliance. Both expect to cover most of their costs for services through fees but look to grants and contracts to cover the costs of developing new products.

During the past two years, NAS has urged the teams to develop these capabilities and provided them with assistance to do so. At the same time, NAS itself moved in ways already described to help create markets for the teams. This chapter begins with a broad description of the evolution of NAS policies governing the Design teams and then moves to describe the challenges that the Design Teams faced in making progress toward self-sustaining operations.

EVOLUTION OF NEW AMERICAN SCHOOLS STRATEGY FOR SUPPORTING DESIGN TEAMS

At its inception, NAS adopted what might be termed a product-development strategy. Developers were selected on the basis of proposals responding to a request that emphasized the qualities of the product and the capabilities of the group making the proposal to carry out the development of the product. Had NAS recognized from the beginning that the product was going to be a service—design–based assistance—and that the organizational capability to deliver that service would be crucial to its success, it might have framed the request for proposals somewhat differently. In particular, it might have emphasized organizational capabilities to manage operations, market services, and provide quality control. It might also have viewed its activities as those of a venture capitalist or venture developer.

In the policy environment that existed at the time that NAS was founded, this would have been difficult. The educational community was, and is, deeply suspicious of business concepts and approaches. The New American Schools Development Corporation was part of an overall initiative that was proposed to be challenging to the educational establishment, but not so challenging that its products would not be used. For example, it was not anxious to be confused with another venture that appeared at the same time, The Edison Project, which proposed to build a national system of private schools with high-performance designs to compete with public schools. Perhaps most important, it is not at all clear that there were many organizations that could have effectively assembled and managed these talents.

However, as development proceeded and it became clear that strategies for providing assistance were important to the successful implementation of designs, NAS began to emphasize the concept of design-based assistance. With this emphasis came two new challenges. First, the Design Teams had to develop the capability to market and deliver assistance on a significant scale while charging fees for their services. Second, NAS needed to develop strategies to help the teams make the transition to self-sufficiency. To a limited extent, it took on some of the oversight and assistance functions often performed by venture capitalists.

In our interviews with Design Team staff, the move to a fee-for-service approach was universally applauded. Design Team members felt that the nature of the relationships that they had with schools and districts was much better under a fee-for-service arrangement than when the schools and districts were getting services at little or no cost. Schools' and districts' expectations concerning services and commitments to change were more clearly defined when those schools and districts consciously made decisions to join with the Design Team. As a consequence, the Design Teams indicate that they have been forced to develop new products and forms of service that are demanded by these customers. The teams have also become far more conscious of the need to demonstrate that what they are selling is effective and to be more specific concerning the services that they will offer.

The jurisdictions found these fees difficult to deal with. While purchasing services and materials is commonplace, purchasing sizable, multiyear, comprehensive assistance packages focused on whole-school reform is not.[3] They have normally sought grants to support changes of the level sought by NAS and its teams. The services they do buy are purchased in smaller lots and often serve many schools simultaneously. For example, they may contract with a vendor to assist in training teachers across the district when they buy a new curriculum and instruction package. Consultants may be hired to provide training to principals and site councils on site-based management. While the total expenditures for these activities may be

---

[3]Most of the Design Teams charge about $40,000 to 50,000 a year for a typical school. RAND's analysis of resources associated with implementing the designs suggests that this is perhaps a quarter of the total costs of the reform when the time of teachers and school personnel dedicated to design implementation are accounted for. RAND's analysis of resources for design-based assistance will be published in early 1998.

sizable, decisions in most districts are fragmented and distributed across many parts of the organization.

The penetration of NAS designs in the initial jurisdiction is shown in Table 4.1.[4] With the penetrations shown, the resources required to pay for implementation appear to have been modest relative to district funding for other services and materials. Thus, in many cases, such expenditures could be met without large displacements of other purchases. Several of the jurisdictions relied upon outside grants to defray the Design Teams' fees. Still, districts talked of the difficulties they faced finding the funds needed.

However, as the proportion of schools in a district implementing NAS designs rises to 30 percent or more, a district will be forced to reallocate funds from other, traditional activities unless it can increase its external funding. Table 4.2, describing the level of NAS activities in the fall of 1997, indicates that such penetration rates are reaching these levels in several jurisdictions. To deal with the demands for funds in additional, newly implementing schools, one

Table 4.1

Number of Schools Implementing NAS Designs, 1995–96
(by jurisdiction)

Jurisdiction	New American Schools	Total Schools	Penetration (%)
Cincinnati	13	79	16
Dade County	25	286	9
Kentucky	35	304	12
Maryland	26	632	4
Memphis	28	160	18
Pittsburgh	10	86	12
San Diego	22	160	14
Washington Alliance	24	200	12
TOTAL	183	1,907	12

NOTES: Data provided by New American Schools. Last column is average penetration percentage.

---

[4]The data in Table 4.1 do not include total schools in the states of Maryland and Kentucky. In these states, NAS is working in a limited number of districts, and the 30-percent critical-mass commitment applies to those districts rather than the state as a whole.

Table 4.2

Number of Schools Implementing NAS Designs, Fall 1997
(by jurisdiction)

Jurisdiction	New American Schools	Total Schools	Penetration (%)
Broward County	16	200	8
Cincinnati	20	80	25
Dade County	68	315	22
Kentucky	56	304	18
Maryland	53	190	28
Memphis	58	152	38
Philadelphia	36	258	14
Pittsburgh	18	84	21
San Antonio	56	94	60
San Diego	25	157	16
Washington Alliance	69	210	33
TOTAL	475	2,044	26

SOURCE: New American Schools.
NOTE: Last column is average penetration percentage.

of the districts has tried to transfer responsibility for covering some of the Design Team costs to the schools themselves in the later stages of design implementation, reserving district funds to start new school transformation efforts. Other districts are considering the same policy. This has angered school staff members who do not feel that they can afford to pay for Design Team services on their own and who felt the district had made a commitment to them.

Obviously, when districts contemplate making expenditures of the level NAS's Design Teams require, they are concerned about evidence of the effectiveness of such assistance. The Design Teams have not had sufficient time to produce a strong record of effectiveness. Each is able to cite examples of schools that have done well with their designs and thus make a case that their designs and associated assistance can lead to effective schools.[5] As we have noted, demonstration sites at which the designs are already implemented have also provided important sources of information that districts and schools need to decide whether or not to contract

[5]With the help of the Design Teams, NAS has compiled a report on evidence of effectiveness that is updated from time to time. See New American Schools (1997).

with a Design Team. For the districts associated with NAS so far, such evidence and the attractiveness of being associated with a prominent reform initiative have been sufficient to go forward. However, the future success of the teams will surely depend on there being more extensive evidence of effectiveness.

Because of the sizable cost per school and given the existing policies and attitudes of most school jurisdictions, NAS and its teams can be said to have developed a product for which there is no existing, regularized, large-scale market. For the whole-school, design-based assistance to sell, the customer will have to decide that design-based assistance is sufficiently valuable to warrant changing its purchasing practices. Alternatively, the Design Teams will have to modify their products. Most likely, there will be a little of both.[6]

The mismatch between the jurisdictions' traditional purchasing practices and the Design Team's products has produced continuing tensions. In interviews, representatives from the jurisdictions regularly say that the Design Teams need to pay greater attention to the wishes and practices of the jurisdiction. In many cases, districts would like to buy parts of a design or to have the Design Team train district trainers. On the other hand, the Design Teams, having been charged to "break the mold," continually have to decide where they should draw the line and refuse to compromise their design and implementation strategy in order to satisfy the customer. They are also skeptical that local trainers will be able to maintain the distinctive features of their designs. Moreover, they have financial incentives to retain as much of the assistance responsibility as possible.

As a consequence of these tensions, NAS increasingly came to see one of its important Phase 3 roles as helping to "make markets" for design-based assistance through identifying jurisdictions interested in the scale-up effort and advocating the interests of the teams within them. It has begun to publicize and advocate the type of reform services and strategies provided by the Design Teams nation-

---

[6]After this chapter was written, the Congress appropriated $150 million for "comprehensive school reform," primarily for schools serving disadvantaged students. The funds are intended to allow individual schools to buy services such as those the NAS Design Teams provide. See U.S. Congress (1997), pp. 96–99.

ally. The NAS staff has also worked with the U.S. Department of Education to increase the clarity of policies allowing federal funds to be used for whole-school reform. Each of these actions was intended to increase the demand for design-based assistance.

At the same time, NAS took a number of actions to help the Design Teams improve the supply of such assistance. Each team was provided about $1 million a year for two years to help them make the transition to independence of NAS. Consultants on marketing, public engagement, and business planning were hired and made available to the teams. As they gained experience, all teams found they faced important and common challenges.

CHALLENGES THE DESIGN TEAMS FACED IN PHASE 3

To meet NAS's goals, the Design Teams all needed to develop into reasonably independent organizations that wanted and were able to work with many schools.[7] In particular, the teams needed to develop capabilities to

- Market their products and services
- Price their products in services in a manner that promises to be acceptable to customers and ultimately cover their costs
- Build and manage a staff that can effectively deliver design-based assistance
- Continue to develop and refine their products.

They had to develop these capabilities with designs that the teams themselves felt were not fully completed and at a time when their staffs were working hard to complete the work owed to NAS under existing contracts.

Marketing and Sales

The initial efforts at marketing were briefly described in the last chapter, where the matching process was discussed. With the

---

[7]This section is based on RAND's implementation analyses for Phase 3 and on phone interviews with each team conducted in spring 1997.

exception of Roots and Wings, which had been marketing its Success for All program for a number of years, and the National Alliance, which was continuing its work in jurisdictions with which it already had ongoing relations, none of the teams had experience with marketing their designs. They had not been required to explain what they offered or to make a case for the importance of their services. They had only two years of development experience in a limited number of sites on which to base their case. While NAS, with the Design Teams' advice, had chosen districts that were supposed to understand what the teams offered and have the resources to support them, it turned out that the jurisdictions had only a limited conception and attachment to the concept of design-based assistance.

In the first year of Phase 3, the timing and pace of marketing was largely set by NAS and its agreements with the districts. The Design Teams were asked to show up for fairs and make presentations. With the help of NAS and the Education Commission of the States, they prepared materials that described their programs. They usually followed up with visits to individual schools or groups of schools that expressed interest on the basis of the materials and initial presentations.

As the discussion of the matching process in the previous chapter suggested, the teachers and administrators in many of the schools felt that they did not have a good initial understanding of the designs they had chosen. Part of the reason for this was simply the short time available for making the initial sales that was imposed by the lateness of NAS's agreements with the jurisdictions; part was due to the lack of Design Team experience; and part was due to the lack of understanding by most jurisdictions of the full nature of the agreement they had entered into with NAS. Of course, all of this reflected NAS's ambitious schedule and goals.

On the basis of their experiences, the Design Teams have reached a number of conclusions concerning marketing strategies. Almost all feel that NAS has a central importance to its marketing efforts. The teams most frequently talk of the need to reach national policy and practitioner audiences to make the case for design-based assistance. NAS can do this; the Design Team cannot. They also feel that NAS's work with the U.S. Department of Education has been important because federal programs are a source of funding for their work.

Most appear to value the opportunity to work as collaborators, although they recognize that they are also competitors.

At the same time, most have reservations concerning NAS's strategy of seeking a significant penetration into a limited number of jurisdictions. In part, they feel NAS chose particularly challenging districts, several of which some of the teams feel do not constitute promising markets for their services. They also doubt that changes required in jurisdiction policies to support multiple designs in a significant number of schools can be made quickly. As a consequence, they must face uncertainties about the path of change in the districts needed to accommodate the designs.

All believe strongly that a longer engagement with schools is required before a deal can be closed. This belief is based on hard experience. Most have found that many of the schools they work with did not have an adequate initial understanding of and commitment to their design. The organization and mode of operations of most schools do not support quick but informed decisions about affiliating with a Design Team. Schools also need time to assess the support that their parent jurisdictions will provide.

The requirement for a longer engagement poses a significant dilemma for the Design Teams. A prolonged engagement with schools and districts is an expensive marketing strategy, particularly if the outcomes are quite uncertain. Working in a small number of jurisdictions or compact regions can reduce the marketing costs, but they will still be sizable and are likely to require the time of senior staff.[8]

Setting Prices for Services and Materials

One of the most frustrating experiences for NAS, jurisdictions, and the Design Teams has been setting the prices for design-based assistance. NAS originally thought that each team should have a simple price sheet that could be handed to a school or district. The districts,

---

[8]The marketing costs should decrease if a team develops multiple sites in a geographic area. Roots and Wings, which has many Success for All sites, suggests that schools and districts interested in their design visit existing sites to learn about both the design and the assistance services. The Design Team thus largely avoids the cost of direct engagement with schools while they are considering the design.

used to purchasing services and materials where prices were provided for a training session, a book or set of materials, or a consulting hour or day, wanted Design Team services priced in the same way. The Design Teams had no experience with charging for their services, were initially not entirely certain about what services and materials were essential, and in some instances, did not really know what the services they provided actually cost. Not surprisingly, there was considerable confusion at the start.

Design Team inexperience in selling technical assistance on a larger scale was a significant problem. However, the most important problem may have been the nature of design-based assistance itself. The problem was summed up in the answer one Design Team leader gave to a question in an early presentation to districts about what the Design Teams services cost: "Well, it all depends . . . ."

The actual costs of services and materials a Design Team provides to a school depend on many factors:

- The cost per student or school depends on the total volume of a team's activity in a district. The cost per school is significantly less when a team provides services to a cluster of schools rather than to a single school, because all the schools can receive training during a single visit by a trainer to a jurisdiction.

- Costs of some components of Design Team services do not vary significantly with the size of a school. For example, it does not cost a lot more to train 35 teachers than 25. However, other costs do vary with the size of a school. The costs of coaching are more likely be a function of the number of teachers, and the costs of curricular materials will be proportional to the size of the student body. Stating costs without reference to the size of the school is not possible.

- Costs depend upon the level of customization of design implementation. For example, if schools can choose the length of time over which implementation will take place, the annual cost of services should vary inversely with the implementation time but not in a strictly linear manner.

- Costs should reflect the level of school readiness. Some schools have already implemented some design components (e.g., cooperative learning or heterogeneous grouping of students) and thus require less training in these areas than other schools.

- Because of transportation needs, costs will vary with the geographic location of schools relative to the location of the trainers. Sites near trainers may be served with day trips in a car. Those that are distant require both more expensive transportation and the cost of the time required for travel.

- Costs include both the time that is needed to deliver services and the time the team needs to analyze a school's situation and prepare to provide the services.

The pricing of services is not simply a matter of determining their costs, however. Pricing will involve decisions about how to package the services. In the long term, prices should cover the overhead of the Design Team itself and the costs of further development of its products and services. The latter costs could not be covered by fees charged for services in the near term, so teams had to decide how much of a loss they could finance during initial start-up. And of course, prices also depend on what the market is willing to pay, a great unknown at the beginning of Phase 3 and still uncertain at this time.

As with much else in the scale-up effort, many of these problems are being addressed. NAS has identified and funded experts to help the teams develop pricing structures and marketing strategies. Teams now understand the issues of importance to the jurisdictions and have begun improving their description of products and services. Most teams now tend to quote a general price for a year of design-based assistance to a school and indicate that the actual cost to a district and school will need to be negotiated. At the same time, the jurisdictions that initially joined with NAS have no doubt become better consumers, and New American Schools has learned to present the costs of a reform strategy in a district in more realistic ways.

Building a Staff to Provide Assistance

All the teams have given serious consideration to how they will build staff to serve significant numbers of additional sites. During the 1995–96 school year, most teams relied heavily on staff housed at their own home organizations. Several also used part-time staff that live in areas close to jurisdictions. In 1996–97, a number of the teams moved to hire local trainer-facilitators that were charged with providing services at four to five schools.

Roots and Wings extended a working relationship it had with the University of Memphis. The university provides some of the staff serving Memphis. The Design Team also created a field group in South Florida. Roots and Wings has also signed an agreement with Education Partners, a private firm, to provide design-based assistance in the Pacific Northwest.

Roots and Wings' evolving staffing strategy was an exception, however. For most teams, the uncertainty about the level of future demand for their services, together with the time that their leaders had to spend on marketing, slowed planning for future growth. Staff that had been involved with the development of designs continued to provide many of the training services. According to our interviews, many of these staff were well received at the sites, but some lacked the credibility and skills that the schools wanted. Most of the teams also made use of teaching and administrative staff from existing Phase 2 sites both for marketing and training, particularly in summer sessions. There is general agreement among the Design Teams that teachers and principals with actual experience implementing a design have more credibility and effectiveness with school staffs.

At the time that this was written (fall 1997), most teams plan to develop a regional training structure but remain uncertain as to its exact form. The uncertainty reflects their inability to predict accurately how many schools they will add in the coming years. They do not know the size of the market the jurisdictions currently partnered with NAS or that may partner with NAS in the future will provide. They (and NAS) are also uncertain about how federal initiatives to focus Title 1 funds on whole-school reform and fund comprehensive school reform will affect them.

Further Development of Products and Services

In the near term, the Design Teams do not feel that they can charge fees sufficient to cover the cost of continuing development of products and services. Several have moved to seek funds from foundations or venture capitalists to support such further development. NAS itself has told the teams it will provide limited funding for product development when such development seems needed and likely to result in significant improvements in the Design Team's capability.

However, most teams report that product development and packaging have lagged behind the levels they desire and think are needed. An important reason is that the leaders' time, perhaps each team's scarcest resource, has been devoted largely to the problems of marketing, developing staff, and putting their operations on a businesslike footing. The lack of funds has also been an important problem, and the leaders have not had a great deal of time to develop strategies to obtain such funds. In this situation, product development has been limited to completing existing developments and refining and extending existing products to reflect experiences in the field.

New American Schools' Assistance to Teams for Business Planning

At several points, we have described NAS's activities to help Design Teams market their services, but its major focus involving direct contact with the teams was business planning. NAS required each team to develop a business plan and provided funding to many of the teams to seek assistance in building these plans. Several experts in business planning, product development, and marketing, together with NAS staff, reviewed and critiqued the initial plans.

The teams reported that the effort was helpful because it forced them to set goals for the number of schools they would serve, consider alternative ways to develop staff capability to serve those sites, and move beyond a pricing policy based largely on covering the direct costs of service. From the comments of the team members, we think the effort had another major value as well. When the Design Team efforts were housed in larger organizations (e.g., Co-NECT in Bolt, Beranek & Newman and Modern Red Schoolhouse in the Hudson Institute), the business plan helped focus discussions with these parent organizations about the Design Teams' future position in the organization.

The initial plans required considerable refinement. Nonetheless, the 1996 plans provided important insights concerning the teams' operations:

- In the first year of Phase 3, several of the teams failed to break with the grant-supported traditions and priced their services to schools at levels that did not even cover their direct costs, much less contribute to overhead and product development.

- To survive, all the teams projected a need to expand the number of schools they serve. The growth rates they projected appeared reasonable and were comparable to those achieved by other organizations with similar products (e.g., Accelerated Schools and Success for All).

- All of the teams foresaw continued need for capitalization over the next four years as they add staff and refine their services and products. Only two teams' business plans projected surpluses of revenues over expenses by 2000.

- Several of the teams faced important issues concerning their relationships with parent organizations, including the level and cost of support services and possible capital contributions to be provided by those organizations.

- Most of the teams considered some unbundling of their design-based assistance services. For example, the National Alliance markets assistance related to individual components of its design; Co-NECT planned to provide planning and support services related to educational technology; and Roots and Wings planned to continue to market individual components of its design. Obviously, the goal is to build a revenue base, but in most cases, the Design Teams also see such initial services as a way of entering a market.[9]

- Most teams concluded that they could not afford to work in jurisdictions with only one or two schools. Several have declined

---

[9]NAS's staff has mixed feelings concerning these moves. On the one hand, they are glad to see that the teams are actively seeking products to provide revenues that will aid their development. On the other, they are concerned because the moves may lessen the commitment to the whole-school, design-based assistance NAS sees as central to achieving its goals.

to participate in smaller NAS jurisdictions in which the probability of gaining a sufficient volume of business is low. Similarly, most emphasized deepening their penetration in existing NAS jurisdictions to reduce their unit costs.

- Most teams felt that they would need to seek support for continued product development from traditional government and foundation sources. They did (and do) not believe the market will bear prices that permit them to cover such development.

NAS again required business plans in spring 1997. These had improved substantially in quality but still suggested that most teams would need capital for several more years. As a result of the review of these plans, NAS has told the Design Teams that it is willing to help them raise needed capital. It has also met with most of the teams' parent organizations to clarify their commitments and support. Finally, it has set aside modest levels of funding for loans to teams for working capital and modest investments in new products.

Chapter Five

LOOKING TO THE FUTURE

In five years of operations, NAS has proved to be an adaptive organization. It began with a visionary and somewhat simplistic mission: to design high-performance schools that cast off the shackles of rules and convention. As it engaged in the process of design, development, trial, and scale-up, its vision evolved and its actions began to reflect the realities of operating in real schools located in real school systems. NAS continues to emphasize creating high-performance schools but has now embraced a much more complex mix of design, assistance, and systemic reform as the means to creating such schools on a wide scale.

As we have tried to emphasize in the previous chapters, much has been learned in the course of these five years. NAS's experiences, as well of those of other organizations promoting whole school reforms, have now shaped new federal legislation and policies intended to promote the use of comprehensive, schoolwide reforms in ways broadly consistent with those lessons. Yet, much remains to be learned. The NAS initiative itself continues to be a work in progress. RAND's evaluation will continue to examine and document the initiative for three more years.

In this final chapter, we summarize the lessons we have drawn in earlier chapters and briefly describe planned RAND analyses that we expect will contribute future lessons.

WHOLE-SCHOOL DESIGNS

The crucial premise that underlies the NAS initiative is that high-performance schools have a design that unifies and guides their efforts to ensure that all their students meet demanding standards. A design articulates the school's vision, mission, and goals; guides the instructional program of the school; shapes the selection and socialization of staff; and establishes common expectations for performance, behavior, and accountability among students, teachers, and parents. It makes clear the student behaviors the school expects when it accepts a student and the nature of the work environment a teacher must accept if he or she takes a job in the school. It provides criteria for the recurring self-evaluation that is essential to continuing improvement in any organization's performance.

At its heart, the premise has two bases of support:

1. A commonsense belief that a clear focus on goals and a coherent set of programs to meet those goals is the hallmark of an effective organization

2. Years of research on the qualities of schools that are effective in meeting the needs of their students and the communities in which they live.

Each of the NAS designs provides both a vision for a high-performance school and guidance for its program.

A second key premise is that there is no one best design. Schools and school communities differ in many important dimensions. Students and teachers bring a variety of talents and skills. Communities have distinctive values. Schools themselves have existing histories and cultures that will inevitably lead them to see some designs as preferable to others. Because of this, NAS has supported the development of eight designs and has encouraged schools and school districts to consider whole-school designs developed by others.

While the purposes of a design are common among the Design Teams, the conception of what constitutes a design is not. Chapter Two suggested that some of the designs provide fairly prescriptive guidance and materials related to the organization and conduct of instructional programs. Others provide core principles, guidance for organizational development, and materials to support that development. Some of the teams expect the instructional programs of schools that successfully implement their designs to be quite similar; others expect those programs to be distinctive in each school but to be unified by underlying principles and practices that are common among schools using their designs. Some designers hope that it will be obvious the minute one walks into a school that the school uses their design; others believe that you must probe deeper before you find the principles and practices that show a school uses their design.

For a variety of reasons, RAND's analysis has not and will not address the question of whether specific NAS designs work better for one or another class of schools. As a practical matter, for much of the time we have followed NAS, the designs have been under development. There has not been time for them both to be fully implemented and to affect significant proportions of the instruction of large groups of students. At a more fundamental level, as the preceding chapters have sought to demonstrate, a design itself does not lead to an outcome. Rather, the performance of a school is the product of a complex interaction of the school (its students and faculty), the school district environment, the assistance provided to the school, and the design itself. Even with the sample of nearly 200 schools we are now tracking, it will be impossible to disentangle these effects.

At present, each Design Team can point to schools that suggest that their designs can lead to significant improvements in student outcomes. In increasing numbers of sites, the designs have begun to be implemented. For the foreseeable future, the experiences of these sites provide the best information available to those seeking to decide whether a well-implemented design is likely to help their school to improve its performance significantly.

The term "well-implemented" is critical. A design cannot be expected to play a major role in a school's performance if it is not implemented. Implementation is the principal issue on which RAND's evaluation has so far focused.

DESIGN-BASED ASSISTANCE

In Chapters Two and Three, we noted that our research suggests the level of design implementation achieved by a school is a function of both the design itself and the quality and character of the assistance provided to a school as it implements the design. It is also a function of the character of the operating environment provided by local and state school systems.[1]

Assistance Strategies

As Chapter Two suggests, Design Teams have distinctive assistance strategies. Some start by seeking to help the school's staff rapidly change what goes on in its classrooms; others help organize or reorganize the content and practice of school governance. Some seek initially to work with all staff simultaneously; others focus on instructional leaders. Some believe that introducing concrete and fully developed materials is most effective in making lasting change in school practice; others believe that the lasting implementation of their design will occur only if school staff engage in significant curriculum development activities.

The Design Teams also vary in the manner in which they attempt to monitor progress and introduce quality control. Some have detailed checklists of practices they feel should be apparent in schools and classrooms implementing their designs. Others have broader benchmarks that guide their site visits and that structure feedback to the school. Several seek to engage schools (or networks of schools) in the development of their own benchmarks and assessment of their own progress.

The level of resources devoted to implementing a design is obviously important. These resources include the time of school staffs, facilitators, and other school-level personnel devoted to managing the implementation, as well as services and material from the Design Team. RAND fieldwork and analysis suggest that monetary value of the time of teachers and design-specific personnel is often three times the fees paid to the Design Teams for services and materials. The Design Teams have varied both in the level of resources they seek and their ability to induce schools and districts to make such resources available.

---

[1]This broad observation is documented in both RAND's published review of Phase 2 demonstration lessons and our forthcoming analysis of the first two years of scale-up experience.

RAND's Evaluation

RAND's program of evaluation and analysis has and will continue to describe and assess the implementation of the NAS designs. In the first two years of scale-up (1995–96 and 1996–97), we have tracked the experiences of 40 schools. In early 1998, we will report on the levels of implementation these schools have achieved and the reasons for differences in these levels. This analysis reflects and is limited by the early experience of the Design Teams as they started to provide design-based assistance on a wide scale. The teams and NAS itself have no doubt learned much from their experiences in the past two years, and RAND will conduct another series of case studies of design implementation beginning in the fall of 1998.

It is important to recall that the objective of the NAS initiative is to improve the performance of students, not to faithfully implement designs. Thus, the major focus of RAND's work from now to the end of 2000 will be on assessing the impact of the combination of the designs and design-based assistance on school organization and outcomes. To do this, we are tracking a variety of outcomes in nearly all the schools that began implementing NAS designs between the fall of 1995 and the spring of 1997 in seven jurisdictions. These data are being provided by the participating school jurisdictions.

In addition, surveys of teachers and principals in these schools will provide information concerning the nature of design implementation, perceptions of the quality of the assistance, the resources invested in the school's implementation effort, and the respondents' perceptions of the progress that the school has made. When this data collection is completed, it will provide an unprecedented longitudinal record of whole-school reform in nearly 200 schools.

The data will permit us to examine the progress of schools in achieving improvements on a variety of outcome measures emphasized by the individual jurisdictions. While it will be difficult to disentangle the effects on student outcomes of the design itself, the assistance, and the nature of the school, the multifaceted nature of the data-collection effort will provide important opportunities to increase our understanding of factors related to school transformation and outcomes.

Both resource constraints and the realities of such a large-scale initiative as that of NAS have limited RAND's ability to probe deeply into school-level effects of the designs and of design-based assistance. To partially compensate for this shortcoming, we will mount a narrower but more intensive three-year study in a sample of classrooms in 20 or more schools implementing NAS designs. This study will involve observations and artifacts of classroom practice and measures of student outcomes that are better aligned with design objectives than districtwide tests. The study will allow a more precise (if more limited) comparison of both classes of designs and the assistance provided to implement the designs.

Together, the studies of design implementation coupled with the longitudinal studies of outcomes will provide a rich picture of the effect of the NAS initiative on schools.

THE OPERATING ENVIRONMENT PROVIDED BY SCHOOL JURISDICTIONS

The decision NAS made to ally itself with a group of educational jurisdictions had profound consequences for the operations of the Design Teams, as well as for the NAS staff. As we have seen, such alliances were originally considered because a supportive operating environment appeared crucial to the implementation of designs using design-based assistance. Resources were needed to pay for design implementation. School-level authority was required to implement distinctive designs, reallocate resources required by those designs, and select staff whose talents and professional beliefs were consistent with the design. The activities of the central office should support—or at least not impede—the implementation of the designs. The leadership of the district and the community had to provide the clear signals needed to induce school-level personnel to undertake an exhausting and uncertain effort to transform their school.

However, the decision to seek a commitment from jurisdictions to transform 30 percent or more of their schools signaled a larger goal as well. NAS did not want schools using its designs to be unique and exceptional schools granted exceptional authority and autonomy by a district. Rather, it hoped the schools would be regular schools existing in large numbers. It wanted schools with high-performance designs to become the norm rather than the exception. In retrospect, it seems clear that NAS substantially underestimated the changes required in the chosen districts' operating environments if they sought transformation of 30 percent of their schools. Similarly, it underestimated the willingness of districts to make those changes. However, its intent to promote such change seems clear.

In Chapter Three, we suggested that many of the districts NAS allied with did not initially understand the nature of the proposal that NAS was making. They did not understand the nature of the designs or the level of resources required to implement them. Many of the district leaders appear to have viewed the initiative as simply another in a long string of reform initiatives, albeit one having the prestige of association with the business community and prominent national reform figures.

When it recognized how far the operating environments in the jurisdictions fell short of what it desired, NAS began to identify expert assistance and pressure the jurisdictions to make use of it. More importantly, as NAS negotiated with new partner jurisdictions, it sought to clarify the qualities of the operating environment necessary if design-based assistance is made a cornerstone of a district reform effort.

In Chapter Three, we reviewed what we learned about these qualities from staff in schools and districts. In particular,

1. Schools and the community need to be clear that school transformation using design-based assistance is a cornerstone of the district's reform efforts. The absence of such clarity significantly lessens many schools' willingness to engage in the effort required to implement a design.

2. A district must be willing and able to aggregate the resources necessary to support the costs of school transformation and have the political and managerial capacity to allocate those resources to the schools engaged in such transformation.

3. The district, schools, and design-based assistance organizations must devote the time and effort needed for a school to make an

informed choice about committing to a particular design. There must be an effective process to match schools with designs.

4. The district (and the state) must grant individual schools the authority they need to implement the design—authority both to change school practices and staffing in accordance with the design and to reallocate resources necessary to engage in implementing the design.

5. The district must act to ensure that its accountability systems and the designs its schools choose have some degree of alignment. Accountability systems—e.g., student assessment programs, school-level report cards, and personnel performance assessment systems—provide many of the incentives that shape the actions of schools. Lack of a reasonable degree of alignment between the designs and the accountability systems significantly impedes implementation.

6. The professional development practices and policies of the district (and its unions) should support the implementation of school designs. The implementation of a school design involves the professional development of its staff. District professional development policies that are incongruent with an emphasis on design-based assistance are both wasteful and distracting.

This is a daunting list of requirements. At this stage of the NAS initiative, few districts are likely to be willing to contemplate the necessary changes. Some districts with strongly entrenched bureaucracies may simply be unable to make such changes without significant external pressure. Districtwide school reform with design-based assistance as a cornerstone is clearly not likely on a wide scale in the near future.

Fortunately for NAS and its Design Teams, such districtwide reform is not a necessary condition for design-based assistance to make an important contribution to the performance of students. Individual schools or small clusters of schools, with less extensive support from parent districts, can implement designs with the assistance from the Design Teams. Districts can provide resources and support for a limited number of schools without the major changes just mentioned. In the process of such implementation, evidence concerning the power of designs and design-based assistance will accumulate. If such power is there, perhaps increasing numbers of districts will find it desirable to make significant use of design-based assistance and to make changes in their operating environments needed for such extensive use.

A CONCLUDING NOTE

When NAS was founded, designs for schools were viewed as its major product. A correlate of such a view was that designs should be put to a test so that it could be said that they were "proven." The test would be provided by an evaluation that studied schools implementing designs, checked whether the design was implemented, and measured the performance of students who had been through schools with well-implemented designs.

The evolution of the NAS initiative described in this report suggests that this view of the feasibility of "proving" the designs is too simplistic. Few proposals, submitted or chosen, promised designs that were so clearly specified that it would be possible to easily gauge their implementation. Experience with even the more concretely specified designs suggests that an important contributor to the likely performance of a school is the assistance that schools receive in implementing the designs. As NAS moved to scale-up the designs in a number of districts, the importance of the school readiness and leadership, district policies, and district political environments became more apparent. The performance of a school would clearly be a function of the design, the assistance received as it was implemented, the nature of the school itself, and a variety of qualities of a district's operating environment. Attributing a school outcome to the design alone is clearly inappropriate.

RAND's evaluation has been designed to produce information concerning the overall impact of the NAS initiative, largely as it unfolded in its first five years. It will provide both policymakers and NAS's backers with a picture of outcomes that have been achieved and the reasons for successes and failures. This is important information that has consistently been sought by the board of directors of NAS as it has tried to determine whether the organization has "made a difference." They have viewed such information as an important legacy of the entire effort.

Important as this information may be, however, it will not deal with arguably the most important contribution the NAS initiative has made. The initiative has helped focus policymaking attention on whole-school reform and created or enhanced a set of organizations that possess the incentive and knowledge to help schools to achieve such reform. Assessing the value of this contribution is work for the future.

OVERVIEW OF RAND EVALUATION FOR NEW AMERICAN SCHOOLS

The RAND evaluation for NAS draws upon a number of distinct data-collection activities:

- Assessments of implementation experiences in Phase 2 and Phase 3 were based on multiple site visits to approximately 70 schools and interviews with district personnel in 8 districts and states.

- A "tracking study" is based on surveys and jurisdiction data related to most schools initiating implementation of a design in seven districts during Phase 3 (fall 1995 to spring 1997). Data include annual surveys of all teachers in approximately 175 schools, phone interviews with principals of each school, and data the jurisdiction collects on student characteristics and performance.

- An analysis of resources used to implement designs in 58 schools during the 1996–97 school year was based on interviews with principals in those schools, district personnel, and the Design Teams.

- Regular interviews with the Design Teams over the past five years for the implementation and cost studies. More recently, the interviews have dealt with the moves the Design Teams are making from dependence on NAS.

- As a part of its role as an analytically based advisor, RAND has participated in planning activities of NAS from its beginning.

- Small, topical surveys have been conducted to investigate areas not covered by the larger research efforts (e.g., a phone and field survey to learn about the matching process in several jurisdictions).

Over the next three years, RAND will continue to track performance outcomes in schools in seven jurisdictions that began to use the designs in 1995–96 or 1996–97. It will also continue to survey teachers and principals in these schools to learn the effects they perceive the initiative has had on their schools. Interviews with policymakers in jurisdiction will be continued to help us follow and understand the changes in jurisdiction operating environments that are occurring as the NAS initiative unfolds.

A study of changes in classroom behaviors associated with the implementation of the designs will also be initiated in 1997–98 to complement the broad tracking study mentioned above. In 1998–99, RAND will initiate a new study of implementation using a number of school-level case studies.

DESIGN TEAM DESCRIPTIONS

ATLAS COMMUNITIES

The ATLAS design centers on pathways—groups of schools made up of high schools and the elementary and middle schools that feed into them. Teams of teachers from each pathway work together to design curriculum and assessments based on locally defined standards. The teachers in each pathway collaborate with parents and administrators to set and maintain sound management and academic policies, ultimately resulting in improved student performance.

CO-NECT SCHOOLS

Assisting schools in creating and managing their own high-tech equipment and network, Co-NECT uses technology to enhance every aspect of teaching, learning, professional development, and school management. Co-NECT schools are organized around small clusters of students who are taught by a cross-disciplinary team. Most students stay in the same cluster for at least two years. Teaching and learning revolve around interdisciplinary projects that promote critical skills and academic understanding, as well as integrating technology.

EXPEDITIONARY LEARNING OUTWARD BOUND

Built on 10 design principals, Expeditionary Learning Outward Bound (ELOB) operates on the belief that learning is an expedition into the unknown. ELOB draws on the power of purposeful, intellectual investigations—called learning expeditions—to improve student achievement and build character. Learning expeditions are long-term, academically rigorous, interdisciplinary studies that require students to work inside and outside the classroom. In ELOB schools, students and teachers stay together for more than one year, teachers work collaboratively, and tracking is eliminated.

MODERN RED SCHOOLHOUSE INSTITUTE

This design strives to help all students achieve high standards through the construction of a standards-driven curriculum, use of traditional and performance-based assessments, establishment of effective organizational patterns and professional development programs, and implementation of effective community involvement strategies. Students master a rigorous curriculum, develop character, and promote the principles of democratic government. These elements of the traditional red schoolhouse are combined with a high level of flexibility in organizing instruction and deploying resources, use of innovative teaching methodologies, student groupings for continuous progress, and advanced technology as a learning and instructional management tool.

NATIONAL ALLIANCE FOR RESTRUCTURING EDUCATION

This partnership of schools, districts, states, and leading national organizations works to change the education system from classroom to state house through a five-point set of priorities. Known as "design tasks," they are standards and assessments, learning environments, high-performance management, community services and supports, and public engagement. The National Alliance seeks to enable all graduating high school students to attain the Certificate of Initial Mastery, a credential representing a high standard of academic accomplishment.

PURPOSE-CENTERED EDUCATION©: AUDREY COHEN COLLEGE

The Audrey Cohen College system of education focuses student learning on the study and achievement of meaningful "Purposes" for each semester's academic goals. Students achieve their Purposes by using their knowledge and skills to plan, carry out, and evaluate a Constructive Action to benefit the community and the larger world. Leadership is emphasized, and students are expected to meet high academic standards.

ROOTS AND WINGS

This elementary school design builds on the widely used Success for All reading program and incorporates science, history, and mathematics to achieve a comprehensive academic program. The premise of the design is that schools must do whatever it takes to make sure all students succeed. To this end, Roots and Wings schools provide at-risk students with tutors, family support, and a variety of other services. While the "roots" of the design refer to mastery of the basics, the "wings" represent advanced accomplishments that students achieve through interdisciplinary projects and a challenging curriculum provided by the design.

URBAN LEARNING CENTERS

The Urban Learning Centers (ULC) design is a comprehensive K–12 model for urban schools. The curriculum and instruction are designed to ensure that all students are taught in a K–12 community, enabling new strategies to overcome barriers by addressing the health and well-being of students and their families. Governance and management also are restructured to engage community members in decisionmaking and to ensure that the design can improve and evolve. ULC also incorporates the extensive use of advanced technology as an essential element for implementation of the design.

REFERENCES

Ambach, Gordon, "The Essential Federal Role," in *Voices from the Field: 30 Expert Opinions on America 2000, The Bush Administration Strategy to "Reinvent" America's Schools*, Washington D.C.: The William T. Grant Foundation on Work, Family, and Citizenship and the Institute for Educational Leadership, 1991, pp. 39–40.

Argyris, Chris, and Donald A. Schon, *Organizational Learning: A Theory of Action Perspective*, Reading, MA: Addison-Wesley, 1978.

_____, *Organizational Learning II: Theory, Method, and Practice*, Reading, MA: Addison-Wesley, 1996.

Berman, Paul, and M. W. McLaughlin, *Federal Programs Supporting Educational Change*: Vol. VIII, *Implementing and Sustaining Innovations*, Santa Monica, Calif.: RAND, R-1589/8-HEW, 1978.

Bimber, Bruce A., The Decentralization Mirage: Comparing Decisionmaking Arrangements in Four High Schools, Santa Monica, Calif.: RAND, MR-459-GGF/LE, 1994.

Bodilly, Susan, *Lessons from New American Schools Development Corporation's Demonstration Phase*, Santa Monica, Calif.: RAND, MR-729-NASDC, 1996.

Bodilly, Susan, et al., *Designing New American Schools: Baseline Observations on Nine Design Teams*, Santa Monica, Calif.: RAND, MR-598-NASDC, 1995.

Edmonds, Ronald R., "Effective Schools for the Urban Poor," *Educational Leadership*, Vol. 37, 1979, pp. 15–27.

Expeditionary Learning Outward Bound, *Core Practice Benchmarks,* Garrison, N.Y., 1998.

Hannaway, Jane, and Lee S. Sproull, "Who's Running the Show? Coordination and Control in Educational Organizations," *Administrators Notebook,* Vol. 27, No. 9, 1978–79.

Hannaway, Jane, and Martin Carnoy, eds., *Decentralization and School Improvement: Can We Fulfill the Promise?* San Francisco, Calif.: Jossey-Bass, 1993.

Haslam, M. Bruce, *How to Rebuild a Local Professional Development Infrastructure,* Arlington, Va.: New American Schools, 1997.

Hill, Paul T., *How to Create Incentives for Design-Based Schools,* Arlington, Va.: New American Schools, 1997.

Hill, Paul T., and Josephine Bonan, *Decentralization and Accountability in Public Education,* Santa Monica, Calif.: RAND, R-4066-MCF/IET, 1991.

Hill, Paul T., and Jackie Kimbrough, *Problems of Implementing Multiple Categorical Education Programs,* Santa Monica, Calif.: RAND, 1983.

Hirsch, E. D, Cultural Literacy: What Every American Needs to Know, New York: Vintage Books, 1988.

Holdren, John, and E. D. Hirsch, eds., *What Your First Grader Needs to Know: Fundamentals of a Good First-Grade Education* (Core Knowledge Series, No. 1), New York: Doubleday, 1997.

Kirst, Michael, "Toward a Focused Research Agenda," in *Voices from the Field: 30 Expert Opinions on America 2000, The Bush Administration Strategy to "Reinvent" America's Schools,* Washington D.C.: The William T. Grant Foundation on Work, Family, and Citizenship and the Institute for Educational Leadership, 1991, p. 38.

McLaughlin, M. W., "The Rand Change Agent Study Revisited: Macro Perspectives and Micro Realities," *Educational Researcher,* Vol. 19, No. 9, December 1990, pp. 11–16.

Miles, Matthew B., "Foreword," in Thomas R. Guskey and Michael Huberman, eds., *Professional Development in Education: New Paradigms & Practices*, New York: Teachers College Press, 1995.

Mitchell, Karen J., *Reforming and Conforming: NASDC Principals Discuss School Accountability*, Santa Monica, Calif.: RAND, MR-716-NASDC, 1996.

New American Schools, Demonstrating Progress: Profiles of New American Schools Demonstration Sites, Arlington, Va., Fall 1996.

New American Schools, *Working Towards Excellence: Early Indicators from Schools Implementing New American Schools Designs*, Arlington, Va., September 1997.

New American Schools Development Corporation (NASDC), *Designs for a New Generation of American Schools: A Request for Proposals*, Arlington, Va., October 1991.

Newmann, Fred M., ed., *Student Engagement and Achievement in American Secondary Schools*, New York, N.Y.: Teachers College Press, 1989.

_____, ed., *Authentic Achievement: Restructuring Schools for Intellectual Quality*, San Francisco, Calif.: Jossey-Bass, 1996.

Odden, Allen, *How to Create and Manage a Decentralized Education System*, Arlington, Va.: New American Schools, 1997a.

_____, *How to Rethink School Budgets to Support School Transformation*, Arlington, Va.: New American Schools, 1997b.

Pressman, Jeffrey L., and Aaron Wildavsky, *Implementation*, Berkeley, Calif.: University of California Press, 1973, pp. xiv–xvii.

Purkey, Stewart C., and Marshall S. Smith, "Effective Schools: A Review," *Elementary School Journal*, Vol. 83, 1983, pp. 427–452.

Talbert, Joan, and Milbrey McLaughlin, "Teacher Professionalism in Local School Contexts," *American Journal of Education*, Vol. 102, No. 2, February 1994; pp. 123–153.

Timpane, Michael, "A Case of Misplaced Emphasis," in *Voices from the Field: 30 Expert Opinions on America 2000, The Bush Adminis-*

tration Strategy to "Reinvent" America's Schools, Washington D.C.: The William T. Grant Foundation on Work, Family, and Citizenship and the Institute for Educational Leadership, 1991, pp. 19–20.

U.S. Congress, House of Representatives, 105th Congress, First Session, *Making Appropriations for the Departments of Labor, Health and Human Services, and Education, and Related Agencies, for the Fiscal Year Ending September 30, 1998, and for Other Purposes,* Conference Report 105-390, 1997.

U.S. Department of Education, *America 2000: An Education Strategy,* revised, Washington, D.C.: 1991.

Weiss, Carol Hirschon, "Nothing as Practical as Good Theory: Exploring Theory-Based Evaluations for Comprehensive Community Initiatives for Children and Families," in James P. Connell et al., *New Approaches to Evaluating Community Initiatives,* The Aspen Institute, 1995, place of pub?, pp. 65–93.

Williams, Walter, "Implementation Analysis and Assessment," *Policy Analysis,* Summer 1975, p. 539.